Nonetheless, God Retrieves Us

Also by Jonathan Bryan

A Life of Love, A Love of Life: Recollections of Our Family (co-authored with Alice Bryan Juhan and Mary Bryan Fuller)

CrossRoads: Musings on a Father-Son Pilgrimage (co-authored with Alex Bryan)

Nonetheless, God Retrieves Us

What a Yellow Lab
Taught Me about Retrieval Spirituality

Jonathan Bryan

iUniverse, Inc.
New York Lincoln Shanghai

Nonetheless, God Retrieves Us
What a Yellow Lab Taught Me about Retrieval Spirituality

iUniverse books may be ordered through booksellers or by contacting:

iUniverse
2021 Pine Lake Road, Suite 100
Lincoln, NE 68512
www.iuniverse.com
1-800-Authors (1-800-288-4677)

ISBN-13: 978-0-595-39583-5 (pbk)
ISBN-13: 978-0-595-67731-3 (cloth)
ISBN-13: 978-0-595-83985-8 (ebk)
ISBN-10: 0-595-39583-X (pbk)
ISBN-10: 0-595-67731-2 (cloth)
ISBN-10: 0-595-83985-1 (ebk)

Printed in the United States of America

For
Patch, Tippy, George, Charlie Brown,
Grendel, Duff, Sambo,
Andy, Lucy, Jessie,
Sophie, Smokey, and Jocko—
master teachers for all who would learn

CONTENTS

Thank-you...

—to Judy for her boundless patience, laugh-a-minute companionship, and steadfast support;

—to all the parishioners and friends who have appreciated Jocko, our yellow Lab;

—to Ian Roberts, whose consults helped keep me on track;

—to Martha Glennan, who asked the hard questions, like, "What are you trying to say, anyhow?" and then gently helped me find out;

—to Susan and Charlie Walker, who guided me out of harm's way on some nuances;

—and to Alex Bryan, our son, who labored through the drafts as my consulting editor. If you could see the stuff he had to fix, you'd thank him, too.

First Quandary

Evidently, Not All Is Well: What Seems to Be the Problem?

Life Mixes Splendid Things with Not-So-Splendid.

Sometimes the Splendid Is Harmonious, Sometimes Less So.

Sometimes the Not-So-Splendid Is Just Annoyance,

Sometimes Grave Tragedy.

Anyhow, What's Going On?

Chapter One

Some Thoughts to Get Started

I was about to turn eighteen years old. My mother and father planned a celebration for the birthday supper, but they also planned to be out of town on the night before, so they left me home alone. Naturally I invited a few friends over. They came—and brought a few friends, who brought a few friends, and so on (you know the drill) until the place was rocking. It was our newly-built house with a just-seeded yard, right after a rain. My "guests" tracked in a quantity of mud that mixed with spilled beer. Personally, I had a grand time. We all did, right through to the predawn hours.

When I surveyed the wreckage, I decided that this was no place to be when Ma and Pa showed up, so I fled to a friend's house. Around noon, my friend's mother sent me home. I really didn't want to go, having some wisps of memory about how things looked around the homestead. She insisted, however, and I crept toward much-deserved condemnation and shame.

My dread peaked as I walked up the walk and saw my parents laboring with buckets and mops. What do you suppose they did? They did the least likely thing—they sang "Happy Birthday" and greeted me with hugs and kisses.

Lest you imagine them weak or stupid, rest assured that this bonhomie lasted about five minutes. Then they issued me a mop, a pail, a scrub brush, and some rags. For the rest of the day I did truly hard labor, but I suffered not a hint of condemnation and shame. That evening they gave me a wholehearted birthday celebration, and in the next days, they engaged me in some serious reflection on the meaning of responsibility.

If my parents had laid condemnation and shame on me, do you suppose I would have remembered this episode all these years, let alone bother to mention it?

The Main Ideas and Purposes of This Book

I mention it now because it illustrates the concept expressed in the word nonetheless. I violated their trust and damaged our house; nonetheless, they welcomed me home and celebrated the anniversary of my birth. They also demanded that I repair the damage, and they used my irresponsibility as a teaching moment. But the primary feature of this episode remains what I am calling a nonetheless response.

The nonetheless response is one of my main concerns in this book. Another is the question, "What do we mean by the term God?" And a third is to develop the idea that God retrieves us. I want to explore these because they address the various attitudes I have heard people express about their personal spirituality. Some people celebrate rich, full, and rewarding spirituality, and they want to expand it. Others pour out their frustrations, confusions, and disappointments about spiritual matters.

I, too, have had both positive and negative experiences with spiritual matters. They have led me sometimes to indifference, sometimes to inspiration, and sometimes to hostility. Like the equinox, my spirituality has been equal parts light and dark, with dawns and dusks in between. In all cases, however, clarifying the underlying quandaries has led to deeper spirituality.

Fortunately, I have been able to read the work of many authorities whose research and thoughts have helped me in this clarification. I provide you with notes and bibliography that direct you to some of these studies for your own consideration. I hope this book will celebrate your daylight of strong, growing spirituality and illuminate your darkness of confusion, frustration, and dismay.

All you agnostics, atheists, Unitarians, Trinitarians, religious liberals frustrated with conservatives, and religious conservatives frustrated with liberals, read on. All of you who deplore religion's strange doctrines, hurtful dogmas, divisive disputes, and overzealous extremism, and who find that  religion hurts more than helps, read on. All of you who thrive on the power of the spiritual life, read on. All of you who yearn for a life-giving spirituality, for personal convictions about what's most valuable, and for practices that express those convictions, read on.

We all endure the human predicament; nonetheless, God retrieves us.

God

This troublesome word will get a lot of attention in this book. Gather a hundred people and ask them what they mean by God and you'll get two hundred answers. "What do we mean by God?" could almost serve as this book's title.

God Retrieves Us

I discovered the concept of retrieval spirituality in watching our wonderful Labrador retriever named Jocko. He was born in our basement in 1990, the issue of Jessie, our daughter Tucker's elegant black Lab, and Shiloh, an enormous yellow field-champion Lab. Jocko lived with my wife Judy and me until he died in 2002. Reflecting on his behavior illuminated some of my spiritual quandaries, such as how Jocko's behavior mirrored our own behavior, how his relationship with Judy and me mirrored our relationship with God, and how the nuisances of living with Jocko mirrored the nuisances of life in general.

Most importantly, Jocko's passion for retrieving led me to appreciate God's passion for retrieving. That insight led me to recognize that the reality I know as God "retrieves" (invites) us into communion, hence the title and the central idea that I will be exploring.

In the last chapters, I'll discuss my ideas about retrieval spirituality, and provide my answers to two final questions: What do we mean by God? What do we do about that?

Chapter Two

Equilibrium: Jocko's Whelping

As Jessie the mommy-dog labored, Jocko burst forth. She nipped his umbilical, setting him free to expand his potential. All was well.

A bulky boy, Jocko emerged as number eight in the litter, the last-born and the largest. All the pups appeared healthy and hungry. Jessie,  the good mother, licked each clean, then lay still, offering nutrition and security. Judy and Tucker's warm, kind hands arranged the whelps at Jessie's ready paps where, eyes shut tight, they nuzzled her and suckled warm milk.

It was a primordial image, that box full of potential. It represented for me the universal truths of reproduction, nurturing, equilibrium, and harmony. Yes, all was well—briefly.

Chapter Three

Alienation: Jocko's Yelping

All was well when Jocko the sealed-eyelid whelp arrived as a harmless little organism. Everything was very peaceful, but that didn't last long. Burly Jocko, oblivious to a smaller sibling enjoying a certain pap, shouldered in to take possession. The wee pup wailed, but the burly guy

ignored her. Jessie ignored her. The other six pups ignored her. In their world, indifferent self-serving ruled.

In the next few days, the wee pup's exclusion happened over and over. She wasn't thriving. Tucker and Judy stepped in to begin feeding her formula day and night.

After a few weeks, Jessie got tired of sharp little teeth abusing her tender parts, and she became less inclined to go into the whelping box. Finally she rebelled altogether; her motherly love had reached its limits. She abdicated her milk-delivery business, and Tucker took her home, mission fulfilled.

So our two kind women had to fill the feeding void for eight whelps around the clock, giving them formula with eyedroppers. Caring for these helpless little animals became a nuisance; nonetheless, they cared and they took care.

After a while, Tucker and Judy weaned the litter to big pans of a specially mixed slop thought to be nutritious and delicious. Four pups ran to each pan and crowded around for the meal. You would have thought they were starving. They jostled and shoved and displaced and nipped one another, determined to get not a fair share but a lion's share—the entire pan if possible. All survived with big roly-poly bellies, sleeping happily for two hours until next mealtime.

In the next few weeks, the eight little pups learned to waddle, then walk, and then gambol. I hauled them into the backyard for a promenade. They followed me around the fence line. The second time I invited them, everybody fell in, eager to go, except big number eight, the one destined to be Jocko the Theologian. He declined.

He plopped down and stared at us on our pointless circuit. I thought, "Here's no mindless follower." If we go, he seemed to be saying, we should actually go somewhere, not around in a circle. I figured that this one may have authority issues.

From Whelp to Yelp

As Jocko grew, he grew obnoxious. If you and I behaved the way young Jocko behaved, we would soon be alienated from our friends and associates. He ate constantly, indiscriminately, voluminously, and slovenly. He wanted to eat around the clock, or the clock itself. He pooped wherever he happened to be. He piddled, yelped, jumped onto my chest, chewed the chair legs, the table legs, even the drywall, and howled in the middle of the night. He scratched any door that restricted his liberty.

Jocko was a rambunctious, overenergized, oversized, rash, brash pain in the neck. Jocko was a friend to all, whether they liked it or not. If visitors didn't watch it, he'd mark their shoes in that liquid way dogs claim territory and companions.

At first, he was too small to whack with a newspaper, so we chastened him with harsh words in harsh tones. If he was paying attention, he

responded with his chummy smile, raised ears, arched eyebrows, and a big wag of his tail that swung his whole rump around. He was beguiling. In fact, he was delicious. He was affectionate, funny, cute, and…actually, I can't think of any other assets.

His negatives were pretty serious; nonetheless, we decided to call his behavior innocently alienating and adopted a policy of disapproving forbearance. That was easy to say. From time to time, we wondered whether we could skip over the puppy part and go straight to the mellow dog part.

Jocko Comes when Called—Sometimes

Some months later, Jocko and I were walking along our suburban street late at night. I pulled my hood tight against the wintriness and centered into warming thoughts. Jocko seemed glad to walk close to me, so I unclipped his leash to let him trot along untrammeled. Nary a soul was in sight. It felt good to have my doggy companion and good to enjoy the liberty of mutual trust and our unspoken covenant to stay together.

All went well, this soul-warming moment, until an aroma struck Jocko's ready nostrils and jowls, activating urges that kicked over our covenant of trust, luring Jocko away from me, nose down, drawn off into the neighbor's yard to follow the luscious waft to its source.

"But Jocko," I thought, "we had a deal. I unleash you, I trust you to stay close, and yet you cave in to this first temptation, abandon me, and disappear into the darkness."

I whispered commands for him to return—now—but Jocko continued tracking the scent. I chose not to follow him around the neighbor's house, for I didn't fancy answering questions about why I was skulking about in someone's backyard near midnight.

Finally Jocko emerged from the shadows. I whispered cross remarks to him and mused on how readily I break my own covenants for my own self-gratification.

Total Depravity

 One day Judy and I had to run an errand, and we confined Jocko in the kitchen for safekeeping. We left the house, then remembered something we forgot. I went back inside for it. The elapsed time was two minutes. I opened the kitchen door and saw, sticking out from the under-sink cabinet, a wagging tail, a muscular body, huge legs and paws, a massive chest, and part of an enormous neck—but no head. The head was in the garbage bag.

I grabbed the newspaper and swatted his rump and spoke stern words. Out came the head with ears dropped, eyes squinting, scraps of discards hanging off his muzzle, and a sheepish "uh-oh" grin as if to say, caught again, or, rather, sorry again, or, rather, sorry I got caught.

Temptation had again trumped covenant. I remembered the old joke—Friend: "What, another new suit?" Shopper: "Satan made me do it." Friend: "You could have just said, 'Get thee behind me, Satan.'" Shopper: "I did. He said, 'It looks great from back here, too.'"

Most of us come factory equipped with bipolar conscience—dread going into wrongdoing, guilt coming out. But Jocko's conscience lacked the anticipatory pole. He had no dread while going into wrongdoing and, coming out, dread only of being caught. Self-gratification, not compliance, both motivated and rewarded him. Jocko's hand-in-the-cookie-jar attitude showed the limited extent of canine remorse. Maybe he was, indeed, having a heartfelt reversal, a U-turn, or a conversion from depravity to decency. That's what his body language said—every time. It seemed sincere each time, but it never had much holding power. His morality resembled Teflon more than Velcro.

After I tidied up Jocko's garbage-strewn muzzle, gave him a scratch behind the ears, and secured the cabinet door with a bungee cord, I offered the big brute this moral guidance, "Jocko, we're glad you live here. We like you, yes, but try to resist these temptations. You can do it. Just say no."

I looked to him for grateful acknowledgment, but he just wagged his tail harder, drooled in recollection of the garbage, and shook himself, casting slobber around the kitchen.

Chapter Four

The Problem

I reflected on the whelping box stuffed with plump pups and mommy-love. The processes worked well. The environment favored life. It was secure. I thought of Eden, representing original peace, no conflict, no imbalance, no threat, and no anxiety. All was well in this microcosm of universal harmony and equilibrium.

Universal. I'm using this word for things that are always and every-where true—primordial, prototypical, and primal archetypes stemming from the origins.

Harmony and equilibrium. Sopranos, altos, tenors, and basses sing quite different tunes. When they coordinate, they make harmony. When opposing forces balance one another out, they establish equilibrium. I think harmony and equilibrium are inherent in the universe.

I saw all this philosophical stuff in a simple whelping box. It got me to thinking about what happened next.

Yelping as Alienation

What happened next? Original harmony and equilibrium suc-cumbed to negative, destabilizing conditions. Big Greedy, indifferent to sibling-suffering, shouldered out Wee Hungry. Other pups fought one another for milk and slop.

Jocko rebelled from the family walk; he broke our covenant not to run off if released from restraint. He couldn't resist the temptation of illicit garbage-diving. He showed strong self-gratification and weak self-discipline, no give-and-take mutuality, and no empathy for his benefactors' peaceful enjoyment of our common space. Jocko became an uncouth roommate, pooping, chewing, howling, and jumping. He became disobedient and untrustworthy. Greed and self-serving indifference dropped discord into the harmony and upset the equilibrium.

Moreover, nature itself seemed indifferent. Jocko, Jessie, and the other pups couldn't care less about the pup not strong enough to get milk and not strong enough to survive to pass on survivable genes. Jessie, tired of delivering milk to sharp-toothed sucklings, faded away and couldn't care less.

The Whelp-Yelp Dichotomy

So there we have it—the whelp-yelp dichotomy in which Jocko and family illustrate (1) the positive whelp—origins enjoy harmonized equilibrium, and (2) the negative yelp—alienation disrupts harmonized equilibrium.

Alienation. I use this word as a substitute for the word sin. Sin, sins, sinful, and sinning have become such trite words that I won't use them without clarifying what I mean. Originally sin referred to chronic estrangement from God,[1] but, over time, the word has accumulated trivial and secular meanings—even down to mere wrongdoing. The word has lost its power to convey the cosmic agony of our distance from God, our broken relationship with God, and our separation from ultimate reality. It has become exhausted and depreciated. Therefore, in order to name our deep down estrangement, I will substitute alienation and alienate.[2]

I'll sharpen the meanings implicit in these terms as we progress, but, for now, please let them communicate the strongest, most serious meanings traditionally found in the word sin.

A Way Station to Consider the Word God

In the first chapter I began considering the various meanings attached to the word God. It has, no doubt, as many meanings as we have people who use it, hence the terrible confusion surrounding it.

I think a lot of our confusion stems from having two ideas in mind, each called God but each quite different from the other. One concept of God—the one we get from reasoning backward to a first cause—bears little resemblance to the concept we get from the Bible; moreover, various other concepts are free-floating through our culture. And yet we call them all by the same name. It's like trying to talk about different makes of automobile but having only one word—car—to name them all. Without differentiation, we can find no agreed meaning.

So I am trying to maintain strict differentiations. This requires me to use substitute phrases like "the deity of causation" and "the biblical deity." Perhaps these will keep them separate until we are ready to consider them as a single concept—God.

Some Questions for Starters

The troubling phenomenon—when equilibrium so soon degenerated into alienation—appears everywhere in human suffering and wrongdoing. From my study of history, from the daily newspaper, from working with people in crisis, and from reflecting on my own life, I see gross universal alienation upsetting equilibrium, leading to a new reality of imbalance, discord, and destruction.

That certainly accords with my own everyday experience. Over and over I have enjoyed (perhaps you have too) original equilibrium in relationships, ideas, and jobs. Negative forces have then alienated the equilibrium.

Thinking such thoughts can lead to a melancholy conclusion that life means nothing, and that we live for no purpose. In Latin the word for nothing is nihil, as in annihilation. We call such thinking nihilism.

Personally, I have no use for nihilism. But if the answer is not nothing, what is it? What causes this degeneration? How did all this originate, this equilibrium devolving into alienation? How did the universe itself originate? Where does life come from, anyhow? Where does anything come from? What's the purpose of it all? Where is it all going?

For such quandaries, perhaps Jocko could help me retrieve some answers.

What am I saying? This dog was, after all, nothing but a big Labrador retriever—a yellow-white, powerful, drooly, handsomely proportioned dog. He had a massive chest, capacious jaws, far more skin than he needed (as a friend of mine once said, "Jocko, take that suit back to your tailor."), webbed feet the size of Ping-Pong paddles, a tail that could have hit home runs, eyes that could say anything, and a voracious, perpetual, omnivorous appetite. He could inhale a bowl of Kibbles in less than a minute. He tried to eat his basketball, the mostly deflated one I'd kick around the yard for him to retrieve.

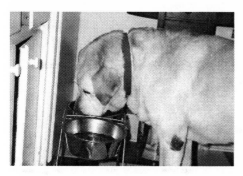

He was a presence.

Jocko's Retrieval Policies

We did most of our retrieving games in our backyard. I'd call, "Jocko-o, find a ball!" and Jocko would sprint around with his tail swinging and his nose down, searching the grass. He'd find a tennis ball and clamp it between those great jaws. Then he'd keep searching until he found another one farther out in the leaves and gather that one in, too. With nose down he'd keep searching in the  weeds, under the bushes, through the periwinkle, into the brambles, and into the mud puddles until he'd find another. Three tennis balls were jammed into his massive jaws. Then he would bring them to me. Once a Frisbee got stuck in the maple tree and he had a wild time getting it out. I had to stop using it because leaping was hard on his hips.

Whatever he was driven by, genes, DNA, hormones—I don't know. But he had steadfast determination to get all the stuff I pitched out there—tennis balls, sticks, logs, a broken basketball, and a tree-snagged Frisbee—back where they came from.

Actually he was indiscriminate about what he brought in. I had not thrown that large limb stuck in the muck, but Jocko would tug it loose, legs braced, and drag it in anyhow. If, as with the waterlogged stick that sank when I pitched it into the ice floes, he couldn't find the real thing, he'd bring back any surrogate.

Every retrieval challenge would be fine for this intrepid dog. Fearless he was, willing to crash into any bramble patch, any icy water, any swamp to retrieve. Go dog, go!

Jocko the Spiritual Advisor

Analogies between Jocko and my quandaries illuminated pesky enigmas about life, death, the Bible, the church, spirituality, and so forth.

I found that watching Jocko could open windows onto the struggles I had in getting useful meanings. I got insights from just having him around, lying down by my desk, streaking back and forth while we walked the woods, towing me along in his harness and leash through suburban streets, drooling while Judy and I ate, wolfing down his food, prowling about looking for scraps, and bounding out to greet us when we came home.

Walking with Jocko

One early morning, I got my jacket. The familiar sound alerted the sleeping beast. He leapt up and sped to the door, skidding the last few feet and pressing his nose against the crack. Out we went. He leapt into the front seat of the old Toyota, then remembered the rule and tried to get down into the narrow foot well where he knew he was supposed to be. But when you're 105 pounds and you try going down headfirst, you get stuck with your head jammed under the glove box and against the firewall, backside still up on the seat. But you're also pretty limber, and finally you get right-side up and you sit on the floor and jam your wet nose against the window.

As we drove to our walking place, we passed familiar landmarks. Jocko howled in anticipation. I parked and fastened his leash to get as much control as I could exert until we got into the woods. He dragged me to the trailhead, and I unsnapped the leash. Off he went on his mad dash.

These woods covered a hillside with five ravines separating four short ridges jutting out from the main hill. Little creeks ran down the ravines. Mature hardwoods covered the area. Trails crossed and criss-crossed, some leading out onto the ridges, dropping down to the bot-tomland, and intersecting with others coming down the ravines. They made a network around and over the ridges and across the creeks, going everywhere and nowhere.

Jocko and I got up to a high point where I could look over the trees growing in the bottomland and out to the Potomac River half a mile away to the east. The rising sun peeped over the Maryland shoreline across the river. The dawn promised insights, Jocko promised laughs, the trails promised interesting questions, and I was ready. We walked on, Jocko sniffing out scents alluring him, I sniffing out sense eluding me, both of us questing. He led me through some rocky spots and down into some depressing ravines, fording some icy creeks.

I got a grip on his harness and shouted, "Go, Jocko, go for it!" and that muscular brute towed me up to a ridge line. Then we sat together, admired the view, caught our breath, had a little snack, and knew the wonder of companionship. When I least expected it, he gave me a big slobbery lick right on my face.

I think of these trails as the topographical equivalent of the quandaries I have elected to explore. Different thought-paths lead up to clarity and down to obscurity. They intersect one another so that thoughts coming in this way can go out that way, leading perhaps back where they started. A trudge up this ridge of a quandary might bring a great view of a new concept but then I might drop right back down into a swampy muddle of conflicting ideas.

Tying Some of This Together

So far we've looked at the first of the four major quandaries in this book. I have titled it, "Evidently, Not All Is Well: What Seems to Be the Problem?" I introduced the concept of the nonetheless response and my notion that "nonetheless, God retrieves us" which will lead to a retrieval spirituality. Then I observed that Jocko's whelping led directly to Jocko's yelping and the universal predicament that our original equilibrium predictably devolved into alienation.

This raises ultimate questions about why we face such a predicament, where we came from and where we're going, and who's in charge, anyhow? For me, what seems to be the problem is that stuff goes terribly wrong and we seem to have no control over it nor any comprehension of why.

A Sneak Preview

In the rest of this book I'll wander around with Jocko on various trails of thought, each with a certain quandary.

One trail will take me to where I have to choose between "no deity at all" or "yes, deity." Since the "no deity" trail leads me to a preposterous

conclusion, a logical dead end, I'll follow the other one, which leads to ideas about causation, the first cause, the big bang, evolution, and the like. These lead to a first-cause deity of origination, a solidly rational but insufficient concept.

On another trail I'll trudge up the Bible's steep slopes to an elevation from which I can see not only the sunrise but also the Bible as a whole, which shows forth the biblical deity.

My final trail will lead to a coalescence of the first-cause deity and the biblical deity, from which we can explore our retrieval spirituality.

Second Quandary

FINDING THE GOD OF CAUSATION

Big Questions Need Big Answers.

Wondering about Origins, Cosmic Realities, Meanings of Life

Leads to Wondering about Deity.

Could We Find a Deity of Causation?

Chapter Five

Causation and the First Cause

Jocko emerged from Jessie's womb:

- Because his fetus had gestated for some weeks there
- Because Jessie's ovum had been ready to receive insemination from Shiloh
- Because Jessie was a fertile dog
- Because she had come from a line of fertile dogs that had evolved from an original canine
- That had evolved from a mammal that had evolved from an earlier life-form
- That had evolved from the first life-form that had found a life-sustaining environment
- That had evolved from physical interactions
- That had developed from various causes linked in an unbroken chain of causes
- Right on back to an initial cause of the entire universe: the first cause of all those physical effects.

Jocko emerged from Jessie's womb not only as the effect of all those physical causes but also as the effect of many conceptual causes:

- Because Tucker had decided that she wanted a litter of AKC pups

- Because she needed money for graduate school
- Because she wanted to become a teacher
- Because she liked working with children
- Because of innumerable other conceptual (as opposed to physical) causes.

One branch of these conceptual causes extends back to a choice that Judy and I made forty-five years ago to marry and have a family, which led to Tucker. Tracing other branches of conceptual causes backward in time brings us eventually to my parents and Judy's parents making similar choices back in the twentieth century. That's a lot of concepts, each of which had a cause that had a cause in a chain extending back in time to the first concept, whatever it was, which—categorical logic in play here—originated also in the first cause, which caused all those concepts.

Jocko emerged from Jessie's womb equipped with loyalty, a human-friendly personality, irresistible urges to feed and retrieve, something that made him wag his tail, and all sorts of other traits, attractive and less so. Various causes produced these particular characteristics, causes that extend back to the first cause.

Imagine the particularity of Jocko, that particular dog emerging at that time in that place. It depended upon these three series of causes branching back in time with such complexity as to make the head swim. But simple reasoning demands that we acknowledge the causation itself and acknowledge that it extends back to something that started it all and to some singular point that had no cause, which was the first cause initiating all other causes tumbling down through time, multiplying effects in exponential volumes till you and I find ourselves facing whatever we are facing, the end results of all those causes. No, not the end results, the continuing results, becoming their own causes. Time, it seems, serves as birth canal for multiplying causes.

Causation

This backward reasoning to find that Jocko is the effect of causes is called the "law of causation" or the "principle of causality." I use simply "causation" and "causative reasoning."

The Celestial Pinball Machine

Causative reasoning works backward or forward. Consider a front-ward example. Visualize a pinball machine with a spring-loaded plunger that you pull back so a ball can load into its barrel. When you let the plunger go, the pinball fires up to the top where it hits a column-pin that bounces it over to another pin. The exact angle of impact may put it high on the pin or sideways on the pin or glancing along the bottom of the pin.

The angle of impact determines which direction the ball goes next and, thus, which pin it hits next and at what exact angle. The angle then directs the ball to whichever of the many other pins it could hit, bouncing hither and yon and always working a little farther down the inclined table until it finally reaches the bottom and rolls back into the holding place to be loaded again into the barrel.

The causes and effects here operate like cosmic causes and effects. They appear to an observer to be random, but fixed physical laws are dictating exactly what happens after each impact. Certain physical conditions are present at the moment of the ball's impact on a given pin. These conditions must cause measurable, predictable effects, such as a precise vector and a precise velocity of the ball as it bounces away. These values govern exactly where and how fast the ball goes next.

Far from being random, all these causes and effects are fixed by laws of physics, and these laws govern variables, including such minutiae as

the current state of the finish on the table and the surrounding atmospherics. The laws of physics allow no variation in the results of each cause.

This hard, inflexible reasoning has the appeal of certainty and clarity, but the world I live in has neither certainty nor clarity, so I get restless and don't want to leave the principle of causation unsupervised. It raises more questions, ornery questions, than it settles, like, "Where did the first cause come from—deity, or nothing?"

Reflection, Discussion, and Further Quandaries

Consider the causation in this event: one clear winter morning I decided to repair the roof of our tool shed, so I set my ladder on the driveway and leaned it against the eaves. I didn't notice that I had put the feet of the ladder on leaves frozen to the asphalt, or that the sun was melting the ice. I climbed up and started to transfer to the roof. My weight projected force down the ladder where it changed direction to drive the feet of the ladder away from the shed, sliding on the now-slippery leaves. This motion pulled the top of the ladder off the eaves.

Gravity dropped the ladder and left me unsupported. As my feet swung inward, I lost my grip and began toppling backward, accelerating until I hit the driveway, flat on my back. The impact dislocated my shoulder. Jocko appeared immediately, dropped a slobbery tennis ball onto my chest, and licked my face. I told him to go find Judy, but he wanted me to throw the tennis ball.

There were more details to the causation, of course, but that's enough to say that every small action had precise causes and precise effects that combined to produce the final effect, a shoulder that still, sixteen years later, hurts.

Now, why did this whole thing happen? Three types of answers: conceptual, physical, and metaphysical.

First, the conceptual causes. It happened because I decided to do this chore early on a frosty morning. It happened because when Judy offered to hold the ladder, I, considering myself self-sufficient, declined. It happened because I didn't notice that the leaves were a slippery place to put the feet of a ladder. Why didn't I notice? I didn't notice because I am chronically absentminded. Why am I absentminded? How would I know? I just am and always have been. Together with other conceptual causes, these provide satisfying, rational answers to the conceptual question.

Second, the physical causes. Why did the ladder abandon me? Because its feet slipped out from under it. Why did the ladder's feet slip? Because icy leaves are slippery. Why did I land flat on my back? Because inflexible laws of physics governed the given physical conditions: the mass of my body's weight, volume, center of gravity, and so forth; the gravitational force at that point; the distance to the asphalt; the acceleration and velocity of my fall. All of these combined to affect the rotation of my body backward before it landed exactly parallel to the driveway.

If any one of those conditions had been different from its actual specifications, the different rotation could have landed me on my head or on my pelvis, either killing me or disabling me. The fall did not disable or kill me because of the precise combination of conditions that did actually exist, a combination that laws of physics governed absolutely to produce that result and no other.

Third: the metaphysical causes. Why, in the grand scheme of things, did I not land at an angle that would have disabled or killed me?

Stop right there. That question begs a prior question: Is there a "grand scheme of things"?

Many people think there is, saying, for example, "Your time wasn't up," or "God still had work for you."

Other people think that a metaphysical agency such as God or deity or karma or higher power or the fates or the gods or destiny or Allah intervenes to arrange for this or that outcome. This idea produces such explanations as "God made sure you didn't hurt yourself," or "Your guardian angel was looking out for you."

These opinions have certain implications. "Your time wasn't up," means that in the "grand scheme of things," each of us has a date with death or disability. "God still had work for you" means that if you do die or become disabled, God has no further work for you. "God made sure you didn't die or hurt yourself" means that if you do die or hurt yourself, God has neglected to take care of you or has deliberately stood aside while physical laws killed or hurt you.

Moreover, these answers imply that a supernatural agency such as fate or God can change the workings of the laws of physics (or chemistry, or biology) to change the outcomes.

In pondering these mystical matters, I also reflect on this fact: On May 23, 1945, during fierce combat on Okinawa, a sniper fired a round that killed my brother, Second Lieutenant Braxton Bryan, U.S. Marine Corps. The sniper's rifle had been positioned exactly right for the round to take an exact trajectory to strike my brother a lethal blow. Those exact conditions were then governed by inflexible laws of physics that caused my brother's death. Was there a metaphysical cause? Was "his time up"? Well-meaning friends told my parents, "God wanted him home." To me, that was preposterous.

These are the sorts of quandaries that emerge as soon as we ask, "What were the metaphysical causes of such and such?"

In reflecting upon why things happen, whether "good" things or "bad" things, these are questions to probe. Have at it.

Once you have settled these, consider this further quandary. When I mentioned "inflexible laws of physics," you may have arched your eyebrows because you know something about physics and I don't. You may know about unexplainable variations in sub-atomic actions and reactions.

I have learned everything I know about these from a book titled *The Mind of God* by Paul Davies,[3] a mathematical physicist at the University of Adelaide in Australia. In explaining quantum physics, he speaks of quantum variations called "stochastic fluctuations." Evidently, certain particles inside an atom occasionally do unpredictable things, stochastic things. They just don't play by the rules.

So I think that while scientists advance our knowledge of the certainties and uncertainties of how things happen in the natural world, we must tread gently in claiming the rigidity of natural law.

Chapter Six

The Big Bang

Ever since people first reasoned backward to derive a logical first cause, they have been willing to name it God or something comparable. We know that Aristotle worked the question this way[4] as did Aquinas,[5] seventeenth- and eighteenth-century British thinkers, and the American founders.[6] The generic term for this approach is "the cosmological proof of God."[7] It's certainly an attractive concept, but it must compete with another approach, which is to accept the biblical account of creation as described in the book of Genesis. (Gen. 1–2) These two approaches have been in steady tension.

In the twentieth century, yet a third approach appeared—the big bang theory. According to a consensus among most scientists, our universe came into being as a moment of immense expansion, a big bang that has been expanding and forming our inflationary universe for the twelve to fifteen billion years since.[8]

The Concept of "Nothing"

To understand the big bang theory you must first get the concept of nothing. To imagine nothing, delete everything—earth, moon, stars, all scientific law, all space and time, and all concepts. Use a cosmic vacuum cleaner to get up any residue; then, delete the vacuum cleaner. But leave the vacuum, which is part of the nothing. You are left with void, zero, nada, nil—nothingness.

The Big Bang/First Cause

So the big bang happened at no time. There was no "before the big bang" because there was no time for it to be before in. It happened in no place because there was no space for it to take place in. It started with no matter because there was no matter. The big bang just happened.[9]

From this nothingness, ex nihilo, proceeded effects, each effect becoming a cause of further effects which eventually caused all subsequent realities, concrete and conceptual alike, including the laws governing them.

Reflection, Discussion, and Further Quandaries

I am interested right now in the big bang not as a scientific event but as a concept of how things happen. In the big bang, reality emerged from nothing. Just so, I have experienced new realities emerging from nothing. Perhaps you have experienced this also.

Consider: An idea begins to take form in your mind. Perhaps it begins soon after you hear something someone says, or watch something happen. Perhaps the idea comes fully formed, or perhaps it starts as just a wisp of thought. Perhaps a feeling initiates it.

It may be something small, like an idea to go to the beach with friends. Or something big, like an urge to become a chemist.

Over time, it develops from idea into yearning, then into plan, then into action.

I invite you to search your memory for such an experience. Are you struck, as I am, by the nothingness of its origin? At some point the idea simply wasn't there. Then at a later point it was. In between those was a big bang sort of happening, when something occurred ex nihilo. Interesting.

Chapter Seven

What Caused the Big Bang/First Cause?

One afternoon Judy went shopping, leaving Jocko alone. He watched her leave empty-handed. Later he watched her reappear, carrying (1) a turkey, (2) a portion of a cow, (3) several salmon, (4) dismembered chickens, and (5) sixty pounds of dog food. Judy and I watched him watch us unpack. He seemed to sense being in the presence of deity. Who was this woman? What a hunter-fisher-gatherer. She must be the first cause of all that's good.

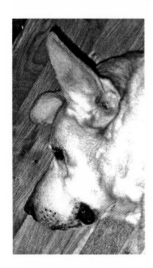

Later, I got out his ear drops, a concoction to remedy the itchy growths in his ears. I made him lie on his side, and I held him down, sort of, while I squeezed the drops into his grungy ears and swabbed around with some cotton. That did it. He lunged to his feet, shook his head, and sprayed the stuff all over the kitchen, including the turkey, cow, salmon, and chicken. Who was this man, punishing an innocent dog? He must be the first cause of all that's bad.

Jocko was learning, I fancy, a concept of a binary deity—two entities in charge of sometimes different matters and sometimes the same matters. From his perspective, he knew only that Judy fed him and that I hosed him down when we came home muddy. He got painful disciplines from both Judy and me. He got led on walks with either or both of us, sometimes with liberty to run free, sometimes leashed. If he wanted to go out, we let him out. If he wanted to come in, we let him in. If he wanted to eat garbage, we swatted him with a newspaper.

We gave pleasure and inflicted pain. We controlled consequences. We imposed boundaries and granted freedom. He could see no limits to our power. He imagined that we knew where he was and what he was up to. He must have imagined that we were, therefore, deity—the origin of all his reality, the controller of all consequences, chief nurturer, tormentor, enforcer, provider; the omniscient, the omnipotent.

Do you suppose Jocko pondered such matters in those long snoozes between feeding and retrieving? Do you suppose he traced all that happened to him back to an origination, concluding that we were his big bang/first cause?

Deriving a Deity

In my early twenties I gave up the woefully inadequate concept of God that I had, in my childhood and adolescence, absorbed from conventional cultural theology. It seemed thin and childish. I also gave up all its corollaries, such as church, worship, prayer, doctrines, Bible, and Jesus. In my youthful certainties, I disposed of all these irrationalities and embarrassing inconsistencies. For some years I lived in a spiritual vacuum, neither knowing nor caring about anything "religious."

But after Judy and I married and had children, I yearned for a substantial, adult concept of God. I sought a deity behind all that is and all that goes on. I got back to the first cause. I decided that the first cause caused everything that we now experience, and I accepted the reasoning behind the big bang. Then I wondered where the big bang came from.

The Cause of the Big Bang/First Cause

This question of the cause of the big bang/first cause brought me to a three-branched fork in the road of thought. I stood at it and gazed down each branch, perplexed. Here are the possibilities I saw:

1. Nothing caused the big bang/first cause. It was its own cause, causing everything else. In tracing causes backward in time, proponents of this view say that the big bang/first cause was indeed the terminal, the absolute end, beyond which existed no reality perceptible in science or demonstrable in mathematics. All causation started here. Nothing caused it. It just happened. Nature was its own originator.[10]

2. The first cause was God and there was no big bang. First God, then creation. This view was the answer for all those years before science offered scientific explanations like the big bang. Today it appeals to those who rely entirely upon the Bible for these answers. It asserts that God created the universe where-is, as-is, in seven days.

3. God caused the big bang/first cause.

When I trace any effect to its causes to their causes and continue right on back to the big bang/first cause, I hit the wall that separates perceptible reality from conceptual reality. On this perceptible side of the boundary lie all the physical and mathematical matters that scientists observe and organize into science. On the other side of the boundary lies religion in a domain with neither time nor space nor any other verifiable reality. But I can make that domain a conceptual reality. I can imagine it and work with thoughts about it.

Since it is not verifiable, one might say that it exists only as a category in logic. Fair enough. But I can name the category outside of space "infinity" and the category outside of time "eternity." And I can name the whole concept transcendence. That's about as far as I can go, and that is where I do go.

It's like Jocko. As far as he's concerned, we transcend his dogness. We provide; he knows not how. We correct him according to policies he cannot fathom. We live a life incomprehensible to his consciousness, distant from his cogitation, and utterly beyond his dogness, that is, transcendent. He cannot breach the wall between his dogness and our humanness. He can observe our human world, but he can never get into it.

Similarly, I can imagine the eternity and infinity of transcendence, but I can never go there, never understand it, and never be part of it. I'm separated from transcendence. I can't prove it. It has no perceptible reality. But people have forever sensed its reality. I do, too, so I choose to accept it as the ultimate reality.

Deity

This leads me to say that the ultimate reality of transcendence constitutes, for me, deity. And to say further that this deity is the originator.

Originator. I deliberately do not use the words create, creation, or creator because these words have become culturally contaminated. Some people believe that the Bible's account of cosmic origins is literally correct. They believe that a few thousand years ago, God "created" heaven and earth, all the features of the earth, and Adam and Eve. We call this view creationism. The words create and creation have become so closely associated with the political discord surrounding creationism that I prefer to stay away from them. So I use alternative words, such as originate, origination, and originator. I'm not very happy with these terms, and I will return to the word create as soon as I have explained what I mean by it.

Transcendent Deity

Transcendent deity has one cardinal attribute, the capability to originate. Starting with nothing, transcendent deity originates everything ex nihilo, provides the "thing" missing in "no-thing," brings everything into being, originates all conceptual reality and all physical reality, originates time when all was timeless, and originates space where all was nowhere.

Transcendence versus Immanence

This deity is transcendent, with no personality and no personal presence. Found only in the far reaches of our conceptual categories, transcendent deity stays out of touch. We conceptualize this deity way up yonder and way back there. We can only know about this deity through raw reason. Transcendent deity is decidedly not immanent. An immanent deity would be present among us and personal.

I have had to learn not to assign human characteristics to this concept of impersonal transcendence. It's hard not to say, for example, that the "transcendent deity decided to originate a universe."

Reflection, Discussion, and Further Quandaries

The line of reasoning in this chapter explains that transcendent deity originated our inflationary universe from a singularity called the big bang. This expansion set up causation leading to evolution and the world as we now know it. The concept of creationism runs counter to that reasoning. What thoughts do you have about the relative merits of each view?

So far, all I have talked about in this book is a concept of God derived by reasoning backward to a first cause. This theological concept is called deism. It has a long history, mainly associated with the phrase "watchmaker God," which visualizes deity making the intricate workings of the universe like the intricate workings of a watch, winding it up, and leaving it to do its own mechanical thing. Deism served me well for a while as a rational, comprehensible, and undemanding concept of deity. Eventually, it wore a little thin. How does it strike you?

Chapter Eight

What Did the God of Causation Originate?

To this point in the book, my reasoning has proceeded like this: we experience effects, which have causes going back to a first cause. In searching for a cause of the first cause, I chose something, not nothing. Since the "something" could not be physical, perceptible, tangible, or even demonstrable, I was forced to go to another category, namely, transcendence. The reality in transcendence I took to be deity, God, the originator of the big bang/first cause, which got us where we are.

Now I will pursue the question of what God originated in that big bang/first cause. Since I want this book to be short and readable, I must either answer, unhelpfully, "everything," or choose only a few important answers that will help us get a grip on the concept of our originating God. So, here are some of the most important things that God originated through the big bang/first cause.

First, I think, God provided the big bang/first cause with what the scientists call "initial conditions."[11] The first of these initial conditions would have been a cluster of concepts, including:

- Ecology: Interdependence among all realities.
- Equilibrium: The result of countervailing forces exactly balancing out one another.
- Homeostasis: The tendency to return to a stable state.
- Equanimity: Balance and evenness in spirit.

- Equality: The proportional value of each element to the whole.
- Compensation: The tendency of a given condition to have a corresponding and balancing condition.
- Symmetry: Balance and correspondence in allocation of features.
- Proportion: Appropriate sizes, shapes, quantities, and other characteristics.
- Harmony: All things working together to achieve balance.
- Accord: Underlying reconciliation of opposing elements.

Call it all, taken together, shalom.

Shalom

Ancient Hebrew thinkers came up with the concept called shalom. We translate it "peace" but not in the sense of an absence of conflict. As a social greeting, it wishes peace of mind, body, and spirit. As a liturgical greeting, it wishes reconciliation. As a goal, it wishes tranquillity in the soul. Shalom names profoundly how the universe originally was and how we are supposed to be.

I think that shalom consolidates all the initial conditions of the big bang/first cause listed above, conditions which continue to permeate our universe. Later I will relate it to the idea of "communion."

God Originated Physical Causes and Effects

In the physical domain, we can easily say that the first cause caused all the scientifically observable and mathematically demonstrable effects, such as time, space, energy, matter, gravity, light and the speed of light, thermodynamics, evolution, entropy, synergy, quantum mechanics, quarks, dark matter, cosmic background radiation, and on and on.

If you start making your own list, eventually everything scientifically observable and mathematically demonstrable will go on it.

God Originated Concepts

The causes of concepts are not so easy to identify as causes of physical events. It's easy to determine the cause of Jocko's bulging tummy (the effect) when the X-ray shows a plastic bag full of Kibbles stuck in his digestive tract (the cause). It's much harder to determine the cause of his steadfast loyalty and unconditional love (the effects).

In my view, the first cause caused not only all physical effects but also all conceptual effects. After all, the nonphysical realities that you cannot measure are, nonetheless, real. Emotions, thoughts, ideas, and concepts are real in our lives. These concepts include truth, beauty, honor, love, courage, and also hatred, jealousy, cruelty, greed, and irresponsibility. Logic says that if we experience these concepts as real phenomena, they did have some cause, and that the first cause did cause the stream of effects that led to them. Therefore, if you start making your own list, eventually all concepts ever experienced will go on it.

God Originated Laws Governing Everything

The first cause also originated all the scientific and mathematical laws governing the operation of physical causation and conceptual causation, namely, physics, chemistry, biology, psychology, and mathematics. The first cause caused everything that operates by discernible, more or less predictable processes.

God Originated Equilibrium and Alienation

Again, if we experience anything, it is a reality. All reality came to us from causes that originated in the first cause, which God originated. So if we experience equilibrium and alienation, they got their start with God. Where else? The implication of this reasoning may jar the sensibilities, for it means that God originated the ill effects of alienation.

But wait. It is one thing for me to put a bucket of paint on the top of a stepladder, and it is quite another for Jocko to come racing around the corner, crash into the stepladder, and spill the paint all over the place. I merely set up the potential for that to happen, not the actuality of its happening. With that analogy in mind, we might say that God did not originate alienation and all of its ill effects but only the potential for alienation.

God Originated Potential

A potential contains the possibility of becoming real. Without potential a certain thing cannot become real. Potential is like Jocko's yearning to pry the top from the vat in which we kept the dog food. He can dream about it, examine it, and sniff it. In that sense, his yearning is a potential that could conceivably become reality. But the top fits too tightly for even 105 pounds of dog muscle to turn this potential into reality. A potential could become a reality, but it won't necessarily.

Now, suppose the feeder-lady or her spouse doesn't jam the top all the way down into the rim of the vat. Soon the potential does become reality because the dog noses the top off and becomes bloated, the feeder-lady and spouse become angry, and Jocko becomes scarce.

Since the potential for gorging was a reality, like all other realities, it had to come from somewhere. I'm saying that the potential for gorging originated untold causes ago in the general potential that God originated.

That means that God originated not the petty larceny in the matter of the dog food—an act of alienation—but only the potential that Jocko would commit the larceny. This puts God at one causal remove from the larceny itself.

Anything that we experience has come about because the potential for that experience existed before the experience itself. It existed in potential only. This has high significance. It means that God originated our universe open to the possibility that anything could happen, anything, that is, for which God did originate a potential. It doesn't appear, for example, that there's any potential for gravity to work backward on Mondays, Wednesdays, and Fridays. There does seem to be a potential for love to  include not only joy, fidelity, healing, and other positives but also, paradoxically, pain and misery.

It also means that God does not cause any of the negatives, the alienation, the calamities that we suffer, only the potential for them. Complex causal factors—physical, emotional, psychological, and conceptual—make these actual.

So, to summarize, I think that God loaded the concept of potential into the big bang/first cause.

A Note on Phraseology

Notice this expression, "God loaded [x] into the big bang/first cause." It projects an image of God selecting certain contents or attributes that the big bang will cause when it begins its expansion. It's a crude image, troublesome because it assigns anthropomorphic attributes to the transcendent deity, it has suggestions of loading a cannon, and it implies before and after timings, which don't apply in eternity. But I can't find a better way to express my conviction that the initial conditions of the universe had certain characteristics—the ones I am enumerating here—and not certain other characteristics. They had to come from somewhere. I say that God "loaded them into the big bang/first cause."

God Originated the Potential for Evolution

Once we accept that God originated causation and potential, we take a short step to evolution. As I see it, the big bang is expanding according to its inherent laws. This expansion involves an evolutionary process. A certain potential becomes real. This new reality makes several other potentials ready to open up if the conditions they require are ready. One or more of these potentials do become real, others do not; they do not survive.

That's evolutionary. If the conditions needed for a certain potential never happen, the potential never actualizes and dies out and doesn't survive. So I think God originated the potential for evolution.

God Originated the Potential for Life

The big bang/first cause evidently contained the potential for a chain of causes that led to the conditions necessary for life to emerge. Eventually, conditions did become ready for this new entity called life. God originated the potential for life to emerge when these certain conditions became reality. They actually did become real, and life actually did emerge and began to evolve. Some life-forms survived and reproduced. Some died without reproducing. Some reproductions survived to reproduce, some did not. Plainly death was part of the process.

Thus does each generation cause another, which causes another. But each also has new, slightly different attributes, each of which becomes the cause of yet other attributes. The potential for life that God originated contains newness, freshness, and originality. Life ever emulates universal dynamics, fulfilling old potentials and causing new potentials.

Scientists are striving to find the chemical and biological origin of life. They will eventually do that, and then we can celebrate scientific knowledge of what our instincts already tell us—that God made life potential in this inflationary universe and that eventually life emerged according to evolutionary processes. Some want to call this a design, but a design presupposes a known end result. In our open universe, I prefer to assign unlimited effectuality to God's potentials.

God Originated the Potential for Humankind

Once upon a time a certain hominid—by which I mean an evolutionary prehuman—went to sleep one night having never had any spiritual sense or thought whatever and having never had any capability to think beyond physical realities. Every thought from the first thought had been biological—fear, hunger, fatigue, and anger. This hominid had never conceptualized anything whatever, such as beauty, honor, love, awe, reverence, afterlife, or the spirits of the trees or springs or thunder.

The next morning, this certain hominid woke up and had a conceptual thought like, perhaps, "beautiful" or "amazing." I think that this hominid, with that first conceptual thought, stopped being a hominid and became a human being.

Let's suppose that no other hominid had ever had a conceptual thought. Our hominid was, thus, the first human. That, for me, is how humankind got started, by evolving a capability to do concepts or, in other terms, by developing consciousness of a reality beyond the physical—a spiritual reality, transcendence. Thus did we first connect—no matter how slightly—with transcendence, our originator God, and our God of causation. That connection with conceptualization serves, I think, as the basis for spirituality.

Evolution had been going on for some time before this happened. In that time, I guess, the ancestors of this hominid evolved some set of capabilities that caused conditions susceptible to conceptual thought. This particular hominid's psyche, as psyches will do as we age, developed these inbred capabilities until they became ready to think a conceptual thought. And the thought came, just like that.

Perhaps then several offspring of this former hominid inherited this genetic capability to think a spiritual thought, and perhaps that capability somehow gave some of them an edge for survival. Perhaps those who could conceptualize survived, whereas their siblings, still unable to conceptualize, did not survive. Perhaps.

In any event, our capability to think concepts had to start somewhere. This is my idea of how it could have happened. I think that hominids—by definition, nonhuman humanoids—lived without spirituality until somehow it emerged into consciousness as subtly as the lightening of a dawn sky, bringing humankind into reality.

Because God had originated the potential for concepts, loading them into the big bang, the potential for conceptualization was there waiting for evolution to do its thing and actuate it as the prelude to spirituality.

God Originated Choice

I have made certain choices in my life, and other people have made certain choices, also. In my view, the first cause originated choice and the human capacity to choose. In my lifetime, I have chosen to do and not to do certain things. I could have chosen otherwise. I have chosen to make commitments to certain things and not to others, to acquire and develop certain concepts and not others, to develop ideas about Jocko but not so much about our resident feline, Hobie-Cat (who never offered much to think about), to learn about sailing but not about soccer, to become practiced in teaching and learning but not in college administration, and on and on.

I think that our capacity to make choices—and the cousins of choice, such as decisions, judgments, tastes, habits, and commitments—evidently originated from God and the first cause that initiated our potential for choice and choosing.

The Meaning of Create

Strictly defined, the word create is used for originating something out of nothing. We have seen that God, the ultimate reality of transcendence, created out of nothing all that we now experience in a way that is dynamic, growing, evolving, and alive. This usage is distinguished from another, which takes the biblical account of creation and assumes that it occurred in a static form with all its features intact at the moment of creation.

Stipulating, then, that for me the word create and its derivatives denote what God has been doing since the big bang/first cause, I will return to using it and will no longer use the term originate.

God of Causation, Transcendent Creator, Beyond "Beyond"

These are but a few thoughts about our creator, God. Thinking about God is plainly not the same as knowing God. A strong spirituality includes a sense of knowing God, not just knowing about God. But personally, I need to be able to think about God so as to get to know God. Therefore I think of God as:

- Beyond comprehension, beyond definition, beyond time, space, and matter
- Not-a-thing, not-a-person, not even imaginable
- Other, then beyond other to Other, breaking whatever limits my concept of God until I get to infinite, eternal, boundless, then to beyond "beyond"
- Not-being, the ground of all being, transcending existence
- Ultimate reality
- The beginning and the end—Alpha and Omega
- Creating the big bang/first cause
- Creating the potential for existence and being
- Creating the potential for all time, space, matter, energy, and thought
- Creating the potential for all science, equilibrium, dynamics, harmony, disequilibrium, disharmony, peace, and conflict

- Creating the potential for all biology, chemistry, and physics
- Creating the potential for liberty, process, growth, and cause and effect unlimited
- Creating all laws of science tightly bounding all dynamics but liberating all dynamics to develop according to the infinite number of contingent permutations allowed within the absolute restrictions of finite scientific laws
- Paradox
- Mystery
- Creator God

Reflection, Discussion, and Further Quandaries

How big is God? I like a little book by J. B. Phillips entitled *Your God Is Too Small.*[12] It goes on in the vein I have outlined above, urging the reader to open up the concept of God to transcendence, mystery, incomprehensibility; and urging restraint in assigning human limitations to our concept of God. What do you think?

What about intelligent design, also known as ID? My discussion in this section opens the controversy regarding this movement. Here's some background:

For many decades, evolution has been the accepted explanation for how life-forms survive by adapting to changing environments. It has been the accepted basis for teaching biology.

Some people find, however, that evolution has serious flaws because it cannot explain every development in life-forms, especially those which they consider to be "irreducibly complex." An organization dedicated to promoting this idea is the Discovery Institute.[13] They conclude that evolutionary dynamics could not possibly have caused such life-forms, that such developments must be part of an original universal design, and, therefore, that an intelligent designer (ID) must have designed these developments in advance to provide for the irreducible complexity. Some proponents of ID call this intelligent designer God, some don't.

Other people think that evolution has been fully competent to evolve complex life-forms and that our study of evolution has simply not yet discovered the dynamics that have made possible what now appear to have been irreducibly complex, non-evolutionary structures. Their solution, therefore, is to continue scientific investigations until an explanation appears.[14]

Some people promoting this view think that God created evolution in the first place. Other people think that nothing created evolution or anything else.

The explanation I have outlined in this section might lead a reader to think that I concur with intelligent design. I do not. I think that God created the potential for evolutionary dynamics fully capable of overcoming all challenges of complexity. Do I think that we live in a designed universe? No. Design implies a fixed end-state. I think we live in a contingent, organic universe that continues to evolve according to potentials with infinite possible outcomes.

As to the educational implications of the intelligent-design movement, I fear for the future of science if the proponents of ID succeed in substituting a designer to explain evolutionary complexity, thus forestalling the investigations needed to discover complete scientific processes. Moreover, introducing a metaphysical factor into a scientific discipline crosses the line separating religion from science, confusing both.

Our colonists came to this land with convictions that European theocracies were insufferable. Our founders wrote our Constitution specifically to protect us from religious intrusion into our tax-supported lives and our private lives. Efforts to impose ID thinking into public science curricula threaten that heritage.

That's what I think. What do you think?

Third Quandary

FINDING THE BIBLICAL GOD

The Bible: The Most Influential and the Most Misunderstood Book.

What Does It Say? What Does It Mean?

Who Is the God of the Bible?

Chapter Nine

Reading the Bible, Whole

One day Jocko was lying at my feet while I struggled with the account in John's Gospel (John 18:13–27) in which the religious authorities are trying Jesus for blasphemy. His friend Peter is outside denying, three times, that he knows Jesus.

Jocko seemed unmoved by Peter's infidelity. I continued reading from a later passage (John 21:15–17) in which Jesus, now resurrected, appears to Peter and asks him three times, once for each denial, "Do you love me?" Three times Peter affirms his love. Jesus says, "Feed my lambs."

At this, Jocko's ears became alert, his face and body expectant. He looked like he was saying, "I like the part about 'feed my Labs.'"

"Jocko," I said, "it's feed my lambs, not Labs." And that big, burly dog gave me his drooly smile as if to say, "Ba-a-a-a-a."

Misunderstanding the Bible

The reason Jocko misunderstood the Bible was the same reason that I misunderstood the Bible—until 1977 I had never read it. I had read in it and had heard snippets read in church, but I had never read the whole thing. It was like thinking you understand Churchill because you've read his quotations in Bartlett's or like thinking you understand your coworkers because you've talked with them in meetings. Miscellaneous encounters out of context yield miscellaneous meanings.

Here are a few examples. In my youth I absorbed children's books that showed Goliath with David's smooth stone stuck in his forehead, David hacking off his head. Another illustrated the following passage: "But Jael, wife of Heber, took a tent peg, and took a hammer in her hand, and went softly to him and drove the peg into his temple, until it went down into the ground—he was lying fast asleep from weariness— and he died." (Judges 4:21, NRSV) What meaning was I supposed to take away from these images?

I had seen artists' renditions of a wimpy Jesus, which was not exactly an object of emulation. Later, I saw Charleton Heston, I mean, Moses, cross the Red Sea. I had heard churchy people use the Bible to certify a point, like, "The Bible says you should love thy neighbor," or "turn the other cheek," or "go the extra mile." These sayings struck me as harmless-enough folk axioms. I knew that the Bible told about how Jesus was born, how Jesus was crucified, and how Jesus rose from the dead on Easter.

Those were nice stories, but none of them impressed me as particularly useful or inspiring. None of them added up to any coherent meaning. But how should I know? I had never read much of the actual book.

Reading the Bible, Whole

By my early forties I had worked out my concept of the God of causation, a one-dimensional, distant deity of deism. But this emaciated concept frustrated me. Figuring that there must be something more substantial, I took courses at the Virginia Theological Seminary in the

Old and New Testaments and read the whole Bible. That experience led me to continue with more courses. Over time I became so intrigued with the concept of a composite causative and biblical God—and the spirituality that it fostered—that I continued seminary work until I was ordained in 1983. From then until 1999 I was the rector of an Episcopal parish called Holy Cross.

Every week among these wonderful, vital people I tried to wrestle meanings from the biblical passages assigned for each Sunday's sermon: hard passages, deceptive passages, opaque passages—merciless taskmasters. They demanded long, hard study and thought. Each Sunday we read these snippets of scripture out of context to people exhausted by their week at work. Who can absorb meanings that way? I couldn't, and I had taught English long enough to know that few people can hear an out-of-context passage cold and immediately get anything out of it.

So I wanted to make these snippets come alive for my parishioners, but soul-strengthening meanings eluded me. Simplistic interpretations seduced me into lazy conclusions. My pedantry generated windy explanations. I found myself dispensing this bromide: "You can't really understand this passage except in the context of the whole biblical meaning." And my bright listeners would respond, "OK, Jonathan, so what is that whole biblical meaning?" I would mumble something lame and slink off to urgent business elsewhere.

This was a very big problem. These people wanted answers. I went to war against my ignorance. In this campaign to learn, I enlisted allies from all over the map: ancient and modern, Anglican, Roman Catholic, and Protestant, orthodox and heterodox, progressive and fundamentalist, high and crazy, broad and hazy, low and lazy. I was no denominational snob; I couldn't afford to be. Beggars can't be choosers. And I employed what I had learned from all those years of teaching English, especially literary structure.

Over the years I worked out a way to read the Bible whole, which let me put the snippets into larger context. "Reading it whole" meant taking the entire text as a structural unit, looking at it from a bird's-eye view, and seeking a central meaning that would take precedence over the meaning of any individual part of the Bible.[15]

The next several chapters outline how this works and how a central meaning emerges. This finding leads, in turn, to what the Bible shows us about the attributes of the biblical God. Then we can put our thoughts about the God of causation next to our thoughts about the biblical God to watch them coalesce into a composite concept of the living God. With this in mind, we'll be ready to work out our retrieval spirituality.

Reflection, Discussion, and Further Quandaries

What sort of experiences have you had with the Bible? Inspiring? Uplifting? Adversarial? Confusing? Instructional?

Chapter Ten

What the Bible Says

Imagine a range of mountains running south to north. Climb up the southernmost peak, take a look around, then hike north to the peak of the second mountain, then up the third and so forth. On each peak you can see the mountain you are standing on but not much more. Go on the northernmost peak, which is the end of the range. It may be an exhilarating adventure, but you still won't see the mountain range as a whole, so hike east to where you can see all the peaks at once, spread out from south to north.

In my seminary years, I read the entire Bible from Genesis to Revelation; then, I stepped back and looked from a distance at what I

had seen—a unified story with a distinct plot. It started with the beginning of the world, and it ended with the end of the world.

Looking more closely, I discerned fourteen episodes making up the biblical plot. Like the mountain peaks seen from a distance, these episodes formed the peaks of the narrative and the high points that defined the plot as a whole with a beginning, a middle, and an end. I found that a meaning of the Bible as a whole could emerge from examining these fourteen episodes.

A Literal Synopsis

In my synopsis of these fourteen episodes, I will state each as a plain answer to a plain question: what does it say? I seek at this stage no more than a literal summary, for I know from years of studying and teaching literary expression that you begin—not end—the quest for meaning by determining what the text says, literally, no more, no less. And note that my flat statement that, for example, "God called Abraham," does not mean that this actually happened in history as literally written. It means only that the Bible says that this is what happened. I am dealing with the Bible as text right now.

Once I have settled what the biblical text says, I can move to the question: what does it mean? You can't get its meaning until you know what it says.

The Biblical Fourteen

The Bible expresses the following fourteen episodes throughout the thirty-nine books in the edition I use, the New Revised Standard Version. I use the generic term Israelites for the people in the plot regardless of their precise identity in each era.

1. Creation in equilibrium—The Bible started with two (different) accounts of how God created everything.
2. Alienation—The original people, whom the Bible named Adam, Eve, Abel, Cain, and scores of others, alienated themselves from God and from one another.

3. Call—God called Abraham to engender and lead the Israelites to follow God.
4. Bondage—The Israelites suffered bondage in Egypt.
5. Exodus—God delivered them out of Egypt.
6. Covenant—God made a covenant with them.
7. Wilderness—God led them through the wilderness toward the promised land.
8. Idolatry—They settled in Canaan, committed persistent idolatry (worshiped the local utilitarian Baals), and suffered dire consequences, including the Diaspora and exile.
9. Grace—Over and over God invited them back from alienation.
10. Incarnation—God became incarnate in Jesus of Nazareth, who taught and enacted God's policies.
11. Crucifixion—The authorities convicted Jesus. Jesus gave himself in sacrificial death.
12. Resurrection—God resurrected Jesus as the risen Christ, a new creation.
13. Body of Christ—His transformed disciples recognized Jesus as the risen Christ and themselves as the Body of Christ.
14. Communion—God has a New Jerusalem for the end times.

Ezra's History of the Israelites

In the 500s BC a high priest of Israel named Ezra spoke to the Israelites to remind them of the history of their relationship with God from the beginnings. His words, as recorded in the Old Testament Book of Nehemiah, are set forth below, arranged under the first nine headings from my list of the fourteen biblical episodes. (The final five episodes, of course, come from the years long after Ezra, as recorded in the New Testament.)

Creation

And Ezra said: "You are the Lord, you alone; you have made heaven, the heaven of heavens, with all their host, the earth and all that is on it, the seas and all that is in them. To all of them you give life, and the host of heaven worships you." (Neh. 9:6, NRSV)

Alienation

(Ezra says nothing of the Adam and Eve story. However, he does weave the theme of alienation into everything else.)

Call

You are the Lord, the God who chose Abram and brought him out of Ur of the Chaldeans and gave him the name Abraham; and you found his heart faithful before you, and made with him a covenant to give to his descendants the land of the Canaanite, the Hittite, the Amorite, the Perizzite, the Jebusite, and the Girgashite; and you have fulfilled your promise, for you are righteous. (Neh. 9:7–8, NRSV)

Bondage

And you saw the distress of our ancestors in Egypt and heard their cry at the Red Sea. (Neh. 9.9, NRSV)

Exodus

You performed signs and wonders against Pharaoh and all his servants and all the people of his land, for you knew that they acted insolently against our ancestors. You made a name for yourself, which remains to this day. And you divided the sea before them, so that they passed through the sea on dry land, but you threw their pursuers into the depths, like a stone into mighty waters. Moreover, you led them by day with a pillar of cloud, and by night with a pillar of fire, to give them light on the way in which they should go. (Neh. 9:10–12, NRSV)

Covenant

You came down also upon Mount Sinai, and spoke with them from heaven, and gave them right ordinances and true laws, good statutes and commandments, and you made known your holy sabbath to them and gave them commandments and statutes and a law through your servant Moses. (Neh. 9:13–14, NRSV)

Wilderness

For their hunger you gave them bread from heaven, and for their thirst you brought water for them out of the rock, and you told them to go in to possess the land that you swore to give them. (Neh. 9:15, NRSV)

Idolatry

But they and our ancestors acted presumptuously and stiffened their necks and did not obey your commandments; they refused to obey, and were not mindful of the wonders that you performed among them; but they stiffened their necks and determined to return to their slavery in Egypt. (Neh. 9:16–17a, NRSV)

Grace

But you are a God ready to forgive, gracious and merciful, slow to anger and abounding in steadfast love, and you did not forsake them. Even when they had cast an image of a calf for themselves and said, "This is your God who brought you up out of Egypt," and had committed great blasphemies, you in your great mercies did not forsake them in the wilderness; the pillar of cloud that led them in the way did not leave them by day, nor the pillar of fire by night that gave them light on the way by which they should go. You gave your good spirit to instruct them, and did not withhold your manna from their mouths, and gave them water for their thirst. Forty years you sustained them in the wilderness so that they lacked nothing; their clothes did not wear out and their feet did not swell. And you gave them kingdoms and peoples, and allotted to them every corner, so they took possession of the land of King Sihon of Heshbon and the land of King Og of Bashan. You multiplied their descendants like the stars of heaven, and brought them into the land that you had told their ancestors to enter and possess. So the descendants went in and possessed the land, and you subdued before them the inhabitants of the land, the Canaanites, and gave them into their hands, with their kings and the peoples of the land, to do with them as they pleased. And they captured fortress cities and a rich land, and took possession of houses filled with all sorts of goods, hewn cisterns, vineyards, olive orchards, and fruit trees in abundance; so they ate, and were filled and became fat, and delighted themselves in your great goodness. (Neh. 9:17b–25, NRSV)

Then Ezra recites a cycle of the Israelites' persistent idolatry, which elicits God's persistent grace.

Idolatry

Nevertheless they were disobedient and rebelled against you and cast your law behind their backs and killed your prophets, who had warned them in order to turn them back to you, and they committed great blasphemies. (Neh. 9:26, NRSV)

Grace

Therefore you gave them into the hands of their enemies, who made them suffer. Then in the time of their suffering they cried out to you and you heard them from heaven, and according to your great mercies you gave them saviors who saved them from the hands of their enemies. (Neh. 9:27, NRSV)

Idolatry

But after they had rest, they again did evil before you, and you abandoned them to the hands of their enemies, so that they had dominion over them; (Neh. 9:28a, NRSV)

Grace

yet when they turned and cried to you, you heard from heaven, and many times you rescued them according to your mercies. And you warned them in order to turn them back to your law. (Neh. 9:28b–29a, NRSV)

Idolatry

Yet they acted presumptuously and did not obey your commandments, but sinned against your ordinances, by the observance of which a person shall live. They turned a stubborn shoulder and stiffened their neck and would not obey. (Neh. 9:29b, NRSV)

Grace

Many years you were patient with them, and warned them by your spirit through your prophets; yet they would not listen. Therefore you handed them over to the peoples of the lands. Nevertheless, in your great mercies you did not make an end of them or forsake them, for you are a gracious and merciful God. (Neh. 9:30–31, NRSV)

Nevertheless

Note how often Ezra asserts the unexpected, paradoxical grace of God's response—staying with the Israelites and not forsaking them although they so plainly deserved punishment for their persistent and faithless  idolatry. Indeed, he uses the explicit "nevertheless" to highlight God's reversal of expectation, what I'm calling the nonetheless response.

Remaining Episodes from the New Testament

We have seen Ezra's expression of the first nine of the fourteen biblical episodes. I move now to the remaining five, which are found in the New Testament. They are Incarnation, Crucifixion, Resurrection, Body of Christ, and Communion.

Incarnation, Crucifixion, Resurrection

In the New Testament we first encounter four Gospels that narrate Jesus's incarnation (Episode Ten), crucifixion (Episode Eleven), and resurrection (Episode Twelve). However, the accounts disagree with one another in so many details that we have to wonder what actually did happen according to these apparent biographies of Jesus. Readers become confused, and some try to merge all four Gospels into one harmonized biography.

I prefer a different solution: to recognize that each Gospel grew up in its own distinct spiritual community with its own distinct spiritual issues. Each Gospel, then, emerged not as a biography of Jesus but as an expression of what Jesus's life, death, and resurrection meant to that community.[16]

The differences among the four Gospels, when seen in this light, seem not problematic but helpful. We need not be concerned about whether or not the Gospel of John is right to say that Jesus was crucified on the Day of Preparation for the Passover or whether the other three Gospels were right to say that Jesus was crucified on the Passover itself. They're both right. John lets us see Jesus as the sacrificial Lamb of God; the others let us see Jesus as the incarnation of God's great deliverance in the Exodus. Both are true.

This approach lets us appreciate, from four different angles, how Jesus enacted God, showed us, told us, and dramatized for us who and how God is. Then we can set about emulating the policies of God as Jesus showed us.

Stories about Jesus circulated by word of mouth throughout Galilee and Jerusalem and slowly spread outward into the Roman Empire. They evidently transformed the people who heard them, for many gathered into communities, frequently at great personal risk of persecution. They cherished these stories and formed them into theological interpretations of Jesus's life and teachings. Eventually, from about 65 CE to 95 CE, they wrote them down as the Gospels of Matthew, Mark, Luke, and John.[17]

Distinctive Features of Each Gospel Community

- Matthew—This community had Jews who had converted from Judaism and were still living near friends and families who had not converted, so they needed to hear how Jesus had actually fulfilled the Hebrew Bible and was continuing Jewish tradition from a new angle, incarnate God.

- Mark—This community faced persecution, so the Gospel of Mark offered inspiration based on how Jesus faced persecution.
- Luke—This community had gentiles who lived in the midst of much illness, brokenness, and marginalization, so they needed to hear a compassionate Jesus, offering healing, hope, and inclusion.
- John—This community had former Jews who struggled to decide whether Jesus was (1) entirely human, (2) entirely divine, (3) partly human and partly divine, or (4) fully human and fully divine.

Distinctive Features of Jesus's Beginnings

The images here extend from Jesus the plain human from Nazareth all the way over to Jesus the exalted Son from eternity.

- Matthew—The Gospel opens with a long genealogy, certifying that Jesus descends from King David. Jesus's birth in Bethlehem is recorded in passing. Significance: his royal lineage signifies that God destines Jesus to become the Jewish Messiah.
- Mark—The Gospel opens on Jesus's baptism. No nativity is recorded. Significance: Jesus's adult presence among us, a human like us, matters most. How Jesus came among us is not important. He is here. So Jesus was "born" when he began his ministry among us.
- Luke—The Gospel has the familiar, vivid nativity scene, highlighting Jesus's simultaneous human-divine status. A genealogy says that Jesus descends from Adam. Significance: Jesus represents God's son, traced from Genesis, to signify his role as the worldwide presence of God bringing compassion and healing to all.

- John—The Gospel opens with language reminiscent of the opening of Genesis, an account of creation through the logos of God, Jesus fully divine from before eternity, to be the presence of God on earth, fully human and fully divine, the exalted Son of God.

Distinctive Features of Jesus's Identity

The spread here extends from Matthew's Jewish Messiah to Mark's Jesus facing a suffering death to Luke's universal healer to John's cosmic Christ.

- Matthew—Jesus represents the new Moses, come to fulfill all the Jewish law and to inaugurate a renewed Judaism.
- Mark—Jesus represents the suffering and persecuted, destined to a sacrificial death of loving solidarity with all who suffer.
- Luke—Jesus represents the healing and unifying power of God, offering compassion, healing, and inclusion to all the downtrodden and marginalized worldwide.
- John—Jesus stands revealed as the Son of God, the divine presence, opening God's love to all who receive him.

Distinctive Features of Jesus's Dying

In each case, Jesus died as he lived, but each Gospel has a distinctive feature. From secure to suffering to compassionate to triumphant, the Gospels all show Jesus dying in loving sacrifice.

- Matthew—Jesus died as a confident representative of a reformed, renewed Judaism.
- Mark—Jesus died forsaken, the suffering servant close to all for whom life is a veil of tears.

- Luke—Jesus died still concerned for others around him, bringing assurance that God heals through loving sacrifice.
- John—Jesus strode triumphant to death, carrying the cross in majesty, fully in charge of his destiny and witnessing to the indomitability of God.[18]

Commonalities in the Four Gospels

With these differences in mind, we can now notice the commonalities in the four Gospels' accounts of the Incarnation, Crucifixion, and Resurrection.

- Incarnation—All four Gospels say that Jesus accumulated disciples and that he taught and dramatized his policies. These include (1) preaching the coming of the Kingdom of God, (2) the power to heal in the name of God, (3) the merits of a life of self-giving and God-centeredness, and (4) willingness to deal personally and compassionately with those outside social acceptability.
- Crucifixion—All four tell how religious authorities colluded with Roman authorities to condemn and crucify Jesus. Several events identical in outline but different in significant details appear in all four of the narratives surrounding the crucifixion: (1) Jesus's last supper with his disciples, (2) his prayer with them in Gethsemane, (3) Judas's betrayal, (4) Jesus's trial by Pilate, and (5) his flogging, crucifixion, death on a cross, and burial in a tomb.
- Resurrection—All four attest that on the following Sunday, disciples discovered that the tomb was empty. All say that the disciples experienced personal contact with Jesus resurrected, although the Jesus whom they encountered resembled the Jesus

they had known in life only in degrees that vary from Gospel to Gospel.

Episode Thirteen: The Body of Christ

Now that we have seen the first nine episodes from the Old Testament and the next three episodes opening the New Testament, we can look at Episode Thirteen, the Body of Christ. Accounts of this appear throughout the New Testament.

Through the resurrected Christ, God commissioned disciples to become the unified Body of Christ, the presence of Christ in the New Creation. Paul compared this to the human body that has different members like arms, legs, and torso but is still unified: "For just as the body is one and has many members, and all the members of the body, though many, are one body, so it is with Christ. For in the one Spirit we were all baptized into one body—Jews or Greeks, slaves or free—and we were all made to drink of one Spirit….Now you are the body of Christ and individually members of it." (1 Cor. 12:12–13, 27)

He urged the members of the Body of Christ to adopt a high standard of relationships: "As God's chosen ones, holy and beloved, clothe yourselves with compassion, kindness, humility, meekness, and patience. Bear with one another and, if anyone has a complaint against another, forgive each other; just as the Lord has forgiven you, so you also must forgive. Above all, clothe yourselves with love, which binds  everything together in perfect harmony. And let the peace of Christ rule in your hearts, to which indeed you were called in the one body. And be thankful." (Col. 3:12–15)

I'll have a good deal more to say about the Body of Christ in the last two chapters.

Episode Fourteen: Communion

The last of the fourteen episodes describes the final communion with God at the end of time. A vivid description of this ultimate communion appears in the Book of the Revelation of John, where we read this vision:

> Then I saw a new heaven and a new earth; for the first heaven and the first earth had passed away, and the sea was no more. And I saw the holy city, the new Jerusalem, coming down out of heaven from God, prepared as a bride adorned for her husband. And I heard a loud voice from the throne saying, "See, the home of God is among mortals. He will dwell with them as their God; they will be his peoples, and God himself will be with them; he will wipe every tear from their eyes. Death will be no more; mourning and crying and pain will be no more, for the first things have passed away." And the one who was seated on the throne said, "See, I am making all things new." Also he said, "Write this, for these words are trustworthy and true." Then he said to me, "It is done! I am the Alpha and the Omega, the beginning and the end. To the thirsty I will give water as a gift from the spring of the water of life." (Rev. 21.1–6)

The first thirteen episodes are relatively straightforward accounts of what the Bible says because they tell what has already happened. This fourteenth episode is anything but straightforward because it is a vision of what has not yet happened. It does not yield well to summation.

What I have given here is my best brief estimate of what the Bible says about the final communion. I will say a great deal more about this matter at the end of this book.

Reflection, Discussion, and Further Quandaries

Remember that I limited the scope of this chapter to only a summation of what the Bible says, with no intent of assigning it any meaning. Does anything in this chapter challenge you or disturb your sense of what you thought the Bible says? When I first learned these things, I was astounded and a little upset. At first I thought they demeaned the sacredness of the Bible. Later I decided they actually enhanced it.

Chapter Eleven

How a Plot Works

Having worked out a concept of God based on reasoning from causation, we are now seeking a concept of God based on what the Bible tells us.

My approach to this quest depends upon a study of the biblical plot. What is meant by plot? How does a plot work? How does a plot yield meaning?[19] Can we arrange those fourteen episodes into a plot?

How Does a Plot Work?

The classic plot has five stages, or acts. Here is a simple plot illustrating those five acts.

Act One—Equilibrium. We come home from a pleasant evening with friends and find Jocko snoozing in his bed. We're happy. He's happy. Domestic tranquillity. A scene of equilibrium and harmony.

Act Two—Alienation. Jocko begins to agitate. He stands up and lowers his head, gagging, showing all those symptoms of a dog's stomach getting set to send back something indigestible.

Act Three—Suspense. Judy throws open the back door. I grab the brute's neck and start dragging him to it. The digestive system is not deterred. It chucks up a slobbery object onto the clean floor. I continue dragging the gagging beast. He continues to chuck up these tidy round objects. In our transit, he deposits eight of them, the last few on the deck. Judy the Steady examines them and announces: "Brillo pads." She dials the poison control center and gets a nice lady.

Act Four—Climax. "Brillo pads? Yes, ma'am, we get quite a few calls about Labs and Brillo pads. Fortunately, there's nothing in them except blue soap. Harmless."

Act Five—Resolution. Judy and I have a good laugh while scooping up the slobbery objects. Jocko isn't laughing. But soon he comes back in and drinks a bowl of water. He then looks for something to eat.

The Dynamics of This Simple Plot

Here's the drama in "Jocko and the Ate, um, Eight Brillo Pads."

1. Everything was just ducky when we got home—harmonious equilibrium.
2. Jocko's illicit behavior and its consequences upset the equilibrium—alienation.
3. We experienced suspense—would Judy and I get him to the door before the eruption? Had Jocko poisoned himself? The suspense rose as we asked the question and waited.
4. We reached the climax of the struggle (Jocko safely outdoors) and the suspense (no poison in Brillo).
5. We came to resolution as we cleaned up, invited Jocko back in, forgave him, and celebrated his safety. This action reestablished the initial equilibrium.

Thus runs the classic five-stage plot, ancient and universal. Watch any TV story and see it in action. In some dramatizations of plots, one of the five stages is not shown but easily inferred. Listen to the next anecdote you hear from a friend about "guess what happened to me today." It will likely follow this standard plot line: the situation is stable, something disturbs it, the tension rises, it comes to a climax, and then it's resolved.

Chapter Twelve

The Plot of the Bible

In order to determine the plot of the Bible, we can assign each of the fourteen episodes to one of the five stages in a dramatic plot.

Act One—Equilibrium (Episode #1—Creation): The Bible opens with God creating everything, all balanced in universal equilibrium. God declares over and over: "It was good." Nothing disrupts its initial harmony.

Act Two—Alienation (Episode #2—Alienation): Humankind upsets this balance through self-serving acts. Adam and Eve alienate themselves from God. Cain murders Abel. Thus, from the beginning, humankind violates the two great commandments: love God, love neighbor.

Act Three—Suspense (Episodes #3–9—Call, Bondage, Exodus, Covenant, Wilderness, Idolatry, Grace): Various episodes cause rising suspense. The entire Old Testament contains stories and expressions of the Israelites' persistent alienation from God and neighbor, and it recounts God's persistent efforts to return the Israelites to communion with God and neighbor. Great suspense: how will this come out? Will God dispatch them all? Will God win them over with love? Will the Israelites' alienation prevail?

Act Four—Climax (Episodes #10–12—Incarnation, Crucifixion, Resurrection): God, communicating yet another invitation to reconcile the alienation, becomes incarnate in Jesus. Although the Israelites hear

Jesus explain and enact God's reconciling policies, they commit the ultimate alienation by killing Jesus. God, however, makes the last and ultimate effort by resurrecting Jesus into a new creation.

Act Five—Resolution (Episodes #13–14—Body of Christ,
Revelation): Jesus's disciples experience the resurrected Christ. They
band into churches. They consider themselves the Body of Christ. They
spread the word of the Word and the New Creation. God reveals, in
Revelation, intent to regain communion with humankind in the Last
Day.

The Plot Tells What the Bible Says

This, then, states briefly the plot of the Bible. It shows that the Bible
tells one complete story. The narrative taken as a whole shows one unified, continuous plot by way of a beginning equilibrium, an alienation,
developing suspense, a climax, and a resolution. It is a unified whole. It
starts somewhere (in Genesis) and goes somewhere (to Revelation).

It's like puppy Jocko sitting down and watching his siblings going
round and round the yard, getting nowhere. No thanks, Jocko seemed
to say. If we go, we've got to go somewhere.

The Protagonist-Antagonist Issue

In considering the dynamics of a plot, we can figure out how the protagonist struggles against the antagonist.

"Protagonist"? "Antagonist"? To say "struggle," ancient Greeks used
the word *agonia*. Greek dramatists liked to show a "pro-(t)agon-ist"
struggling with an "ant(i)-agonist." The antagonist would test the character of the protagonist, the main persona. The antagonist might be the
protagonist's mortal enemies…or a personal flaw such as hubris
(pride)…or fate…or the gods, etc. The plot would trace the protago-

nist's struggles, which would develop suspense: Would the protagonist show the strength of character needed to prevail over the antagonist? Or would the adversaries be too powerful even for a heroic character? The climax would reveal the answer, and the resolution would tie it all together.

In the biblical plot, who actually is the protagonist? Who or what actually is the antagonist? Is this story about God's struggle against an adversary, namely, the Israelites, or is it about the Israelites' struggle against an adversary, namely, God?

(Note, please, that I'm using "Israelite" in its broadest sense, the people of Israel in their alienated condition. Further, let me stipulate that the people themselves are not the antagonists but the way they live their lives, the alienation they cause. This idea is related to that old expression that God loves the sinner but not the sin.)

Now, there are two ways to answer this question. First, you may decide that God is the protagonist and the Israelites are the antagonist. Then you are saying that this story is all about God, the central character. The Israelites test God's policies. The issue is: will God's policies succeed in restoring humankind to communion with God and community with one another?

Second, you may decide that the Israelites are the protagonist and God is the antagonist. Then you are saying that this story is all about the Israelites, the central persona. God tests their character. The issues are: will they exercise strength of character that will save them from the judgment of God, or will their character collapse under the weight of God's requirements of them? Will God's policies thus triumph over them, break them, leaving them at the mercy of God's judgment?

I believe in the first possibility. If God is the protagonist, then the Bible says this: the people's behavior caused persistent alienation from God and one another and God kept on seeking communion with them.

Let me say again that this is, by my reckoning, what the Bible says. We have not gotten to what it means. Meaning must flow from what it says.

Reflection, Discussion, and Further Quandaries

Two readings of the Bible, sometimes combined into one, are widely accepted: first, the Bible contains precepts, rules, parables, regulations, and laws that tell us what we should and shouldn't do. And second, the Bible explains that we are sinful people and that God has a plan for correcting our sins and/or punishing us for them. Do you have any thoughts on these matters?

Does it appear to you that the reasoning in this book is going to lead to one or the other of these? Or neither one, or something else?

Chapter Thirteen

The "Nonetheless Response"

Now that we have some clarity about what the Bible says and how it says it, I want to take a closer look at the word nonetheless to see what it can tell about the meaning of the Bible and, therefore, our concept of the biblical God.

The Paradox of Nonetheless

Which of the following statements makes more sense to you? (1) Disgusted with Jocko's chronic, intractable misbehavior, I insulted him and spoke unkind words to him in a disapproving voice; there- fore, he walked out, lay in his corner with his face to the wall, and wouldn't speak to me for three days. (2) Disgusted with Jocko's chronic, intractable mis- behavior, I insulted him and spoke unkind words to him in a disapproving voice; nonetheless, 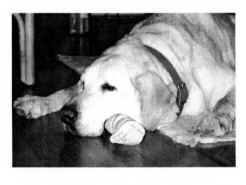 he wagged his tail, smiled a cheerful smile, and curled up beside me, resting his chin on my feet.

I would have expected the first reaction, that of Jocko walking out and shunning me. In my experience, the natural and logical reaction to rejection is reciprocal rejection. Tit begets tat.

But Jocko didn't operate that way—ever. Maybe he just didn't catch on that I was rejecting him, but maybe he had a nonetheless attitude. Maybe he valued forgiveness, reconciliation, and second chances. Maybe Jocko didn't like being alienated from Judy and me. Maybe he was able to do what we all want to do, that is, avoid alienation and offer unconditional love.

The word nonetheless signals this sort of attitude and relationship. It carries meanings associated with despite, however, regardless, even though, and notwithstanding. To express an unexpected and counter-intuitive reversal, you use one of these words.

Nonetheless responses reverse logic and expectation. By contrast, therefore reactions are logical and expected. Nonetheless responses interest me a great deal. They're rare birds, lovely to watch, and hard to catch. Human nature doesn't seem to gravitate naturally to nonetheless responses. They require a commitment to a strange and wonderful attitude. Irony and paradox lie under nonetheless responses.

Jocko and Nonetheless Responses

Jocko drew nonetheless responses from us. Recall that we found his puppyish behavior pretty obnoxious. In the chapter called "Alienation: Jocko's Yelping," I wrote, "Nonetheless, we decided to call his behavior innocently alienating and adopted a policy of disapproving forbearance." And I noted that Judy and Tucker decided to feed the puppies day and night. "Caring for these helpless little animals became a nuisance; nonetheless, they cared and they took care." These were nonetheless responses.

Where We've Been with Jocko and Where We're Going

I've explained fourteen episodes that form a biblical plot that leads us from equilibrium to alienation, through suspense to climax and finally to resolution. I've identified the concept of nonetheless. Next I will bring these strands together to find a meaning of the Bible taken as a whole.

Reflection, Discussion, and Further Quandaries

What experiences have you had with nonetheless responses? How about therefore reactions?

Chapter Fourteen

What Does the Biblical Plot Mean?

One day when I came home, I smelled a certain familiar smell. It said simply that there was a bad smell around here that only Jocko could have caused. But what did this smell mean to me? Only context would tell.

If I smelled it in the yard as I approached the front door, it said merely "bad smell," signifying that Jocko had answered a call of nature in the yard. It meant only that I needed to watch my step. But if it was in the kitchen where Jocko was confined, it meant that Jocko would look crestfallen and try to hide, and it meant that I would have to do that thing that leaves me retching.

Meaning changes with context. An in-house smell has meaning different from an outhouse—no, wait—an out-of-house smell. That's why it's so important to get the whole-Bible context. Biblical passages take on meanings depending upon their whole-Bible context. If you get the wrong context, you get the wrong meaning.

Meaning Emerges from Plot

One context that can yield meaning is plot. Try these:

Plot #1—
- Equilibrium: He goes to work at his new job.
- Alienation: He insults the elderly receptionist.
- Suspense: He miscalculates the sale prices. He denies fault for the resulting losses. He does this each month for three months. What will happen?
- Climax: He gets a pink slip.
- Resolution: He doesn't get another job.

Some valid meanings of this plot include that he has a diplomacy problem, he calculates poorly, and he exhibits inappropriate defensiveness. Although the plot did not say any of this explicitly, our common sense infers these meanings from this plot. Some invalid meanings might include that he had a wretched childhood, he is a masochist, or his bosses were impossible to work with. All these things may be true, but they cannot be inferred from this plot.

Plot #2—
- Equilibrium: The household feline, Hobie-Cat, finds Jocko sleeping peacefully.
- Alienation: He climbs up on Jocko's inert form like a Lilliputian on Gulliver.
- Suspense: He grips Jocko's coat and clings there while chomping down on the skin of Jocko's furrowed neck. Will Jocko leap up and behead the little varmint? Will Hobie take a swing at Jocko's eye and blind him? Jocko wakes up, shows no signs of distress, and just lets it happen.
- Climax: Hobie climbs down and saunters off.

- Resolution: Jocko returns to napping.

Some valid meanings in this plot: Hobie has peculiar tastes in entertainment; Jocko has strong equanimity. Some invalid meanings: Jocko lives in a sort of Zen zone; Hobie gets his dominance jollies this way. Perhaps, but we haven't enough information to infer these meanings.

Deriving Meaning from the Bible as a Whole

To tease out the meaning of the biblical plot, I have inserted interpretive words into the plain summary of the fourteen biblical episodes. Now it reads like this:

After creating a balanced and evolving universe, God gives humankind conditions for living in peaceful, harmonious communion with God—in Eden, or shalom, or in dramatic terms, equilibrium.

Given the choice to continue in these perfect conditions or not, humankind chooses to rebel against God. This alienation starts conflict between the protagonist, God, and the antagonist, humankind's arrogance.

The suspense begins as we wonder what God will do about this: react with anger and disgust and abandon them? No, God stays faithful to humankind. Regardless of their affront, God does not abandon them, but in an act of grace, calls Abraham to communion. God's reversal of our expectation, a nonetheless response, surprises us.

The Israelites suffer bondage in Egypt, but, as before, God continues in steadfast love, delivering them. In a further act of grace, God makes with them an unconditional covenant, and leads them (despite their repeated rebellions) through the wilderness into Canaan. In this fruitful land, a sort of reprise of Eden, they prove again unfaithful to God, committing wholesale idolatry; nonetheless, God invites them, in grace, over and over to return to communion.

In an unexpected climax, God becomes incarnate in Jesus of Nazareth and enacts God's policies; however, surpassing all previous infidelities, the Israelites ignore the teachings and crucify the teacher. Nonetheless (again), God prevails by making a new creation through the resurrection of the living Christ.

Now begins the long resolution. Those people who had witnessed these episodes of incarnation, crucifixion, and resurrection become transformed into realizing that they are the continuation of Jesus's presence in the world, the Body of Christ. They spread God's policies widely, sustained in God's enlivening Spirit. The Bible concludes with God's promise for ultimate fulfillment at the end of time, an invitation to rejoin God in communion.

A Central Meaning of the Bible

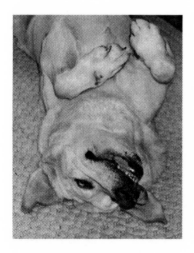

That's the biblical plot expanded to show its meaning beyond what it merely says. We can summarize it into a central meaning emerging from the biblical plot—God creates, humankind alienates; nonetheless, God invites us back.

Reflection, Discussion, and Further Quandaries

How does this meaning of the Bible as a whole sit with any meanings you may have thought the Bible has?

Chapter Fifteen

Nonetheless, Agape

Reading the Bible as a whole, we have seen that God had ample justification for abandoning or condemning us; nonetheless, according to this reading of the Bible, God remained faithful and continued not only to provide for our well-being but also—most importantly—to invite us home. Evidently, God has a nonetheless policy.

God's Nonetheless Policy Shows Grace and Love

We have a word for steadfast concern for the well-being of others: love. But it gets used so much that it loses force. Consider three uses:

1. "I love your considerate and generous nature" signifies love that is only an amplified degree of like and is not really love at all.
2. "I love you when you treat me well—but only then" signifies conditional love that will be withdrawn for cause and reinstated for good behavior.
3. "I love you regardless of your failures" signifies unconditional love that remains constant through thick and thin, sunshine and rain. It's the genuine article. It may be based upon liking but it finds its strength in commitment to the well-being of the person loved, sustained at a degree of cost.

This is where the concept of nonetheless comes to bear. To get into this concept we need another word, grace. We use it to name unearned forgiveness and gentle acceptance of wrongdoing, offered freely in love.

The word for getting not what you deserve but love instead is grace. Grace, combined with love, strengthens the concept of the nonetheless

response. It says, regardless of my negatives, no matter that I deserve rejection, you nonetheless love me.

The significance of the biblical plot, then, is that the biblical God has policies that reflect grace love. I'm glad to know that.

Agape

Henceforth, I refer to this biblical grace and love as agape, a Greek word that translates into "self-giving love." Dictionaries report that it is pronounced all sorts of ways, such as "AH-guh-pe." (But not "uh-GAPE," which is what I was—agape—when I first realized the boundless grace and love that God demonstrates in the Bible.)

Reflection, Discussion, and Further Quandaries

In reflecting on your life, locate instances of (1) love being confused with merely liking very much, (2) conditional love, and (3) unconditional love. Locate instances of grace and love combined.

Chapter Sixteen

Interpreting the Bible

One directive we had for Jocko about entering the house was that he could bring in no sticks, balls, or other playthings. He had to leave them outdoors. Oh, the misery of it, the pain of leaving behind something treasured, the hesitation before coming over the threshold, scheming some way to infiltrate the barrier. If

we happened to leave the door ajar and Jocko approached with some sticks and tennis balls in his jaws, he tried to slip in when no one was looking.

If he did, he got no breaks. While I pitched the slobbery articles back out, I made reproachful sounds to let him know he had transgressed. I never could get him to carry them back out himself.

I did not welcome Jocko coming home with his mouth jammed with outdoor stuff. I did not treat him as the father treated his prodigal son.

The Parable of the Prodigal Son

The parable of the prodigal son expresses, in miniature, the plot and meaning of the whole Bible. Jesus tells it to illustrate the policies of God the Father regarding his children. I quote it here (Luke 15:11–24, NRSV), setting it into the five-act structure that we have seen in reading the Bible whole.

Act One: Equilibrium—Jesus describes a stable household condition.

There was a man who had two sons.

Act Two: Alienation—The son squanders the inheritance.

The younger of them said to his father, "Father, give me the share of the property that will belong to me." So he divided his property between them. A few days later the younger son gathered all he had and traveled to a distant country, and there he squandered his property in dissolute living.

Act Three: Suspense—How far will this go?

When he had spent everything, a severe famine took place throughout that country, and he began to be in need. So he went and hired himself out to one of the citizens of that country, who sent him to his fields to feed the pigs. He would gladly have filled himself with the pods that the pigs were eating; and no one gave him anything. But when he came to himself he said, "How many of my father's hired hands have bread enough and to spare, but here I am dying of hunger! I will get up and go to my father, and I will say to him, 'Father, I have sinned against heaven and before you; I am no longer worthy to be called your son; treat me like one of your hired hands.'" So he set off and went to his father.

Act Four: Climax—Nonetheless, the father responds with gracious love, agape.

But while he was still far off, his father saw him and was filled with compassion; he ran and put his arms around him and kissed him.

Act Five: Resolution—Both father and son have fitting responses to the climax.

Then the son said to him, "Father, I have sinned against heaven and before you; I am no longer worthy to be called your son." But the father said to his slaves, "Quickly, bring out a robe—the best one—and put it on him; put a ring on his finger and sandals on his feet. And get the fatted calf and kill it, and let us eat and celebrate; for this son of mine was dead and is alive again; he was lost and is found!" And they began to celebrate.

(The remainder of this parable, concerning the elder son, while an integral part of Jesus's teaching, serves to begin another drama, which has its own meaning. I'll leave that for another time.)

The Parallel between the Parable and the Bible

To summarize the plot of this parable: the father has made a stable household, but the younger son alienates himself from it and from the father; nonetheless, the father yearns for the son's return, and welcomes him back with a celebration.

That clearly parallels the plot of the Bible: God created all in equilibrium, but humankind alienated themselves from God and one another; nonetheless, God invited humankind to return to communion. Just as the father enacted nonetheless love for the prodigal, so does God have nonetheless love, agape, for humankind.

That's interesting. Is it more than interesting? Does it have significance for the way I live? Does it make any difference? Or is it merely interesting? Well, I think it's merely interesting unless it provides direction for living my life.

Love God...Love Self...Love neighbor

So the more I think about it, the more I get drawn to what Jesus did and said. He not only demonstrated agape, he said something about agape that does offer direction for living: "You shall love the Lord your God with all your heart, and with all your soul, and with all your strength, and with all your mind; and your neighbor as yourself." (Luke 10:27) Since he quotes it from the Old Testament, and since he validates it with his highest rating, and since he is who he is, those few words show me this:

Yes, God created all in equilibrium and yes, humankind alienated themselves from God and one another, and yes, God nonetheless invited humankind to return to communion; therefore yes, I can think of but one fitting response to this extraordinary gift of agape: love God…love self…love neighbor.

There it is. The gold standard. A biblical conclusion that can give direction to life. I could adopt it as my own spiritual constitution.

Reflection, Discussion, and Further Quandaries

Consider the parable of Jocko, the dog who looked everywhere except where it was.

One fall afternoon I was raking leaves and Jocko bounded up to me with a stick clamped between his jaws. He romped around, teasing me. He dropped the stick at my feet and smiled up as if to say, do your duty, boss. Pitch it out there. But I was on deadline. I kept raking. He was so insistent and such a nuisance, however, that finally I picked it up and heaved it as far as I could into the brambles along the fence line.

Off he went at a gallop and with about four yards to go slammed on the brakes like sliding into home plate. His paws caught in the vines and over he went, skidding the last few yards on his side, or chin, rolling entirely over. He fetched up right at the stick, struggling upright, gripping it in the mighty jaws, and scrambled back toward me, legs churning around like one of those cartoon characters. Now here he came, triumphant, ears flapping, eyes gleaming, tail sweeping through 270 degrees, prancing home to drop it.

Well, he seemed to say, that was fun, but it's time to go again, and you don't really think that raking leaves is more important than proving out our retrieval spirituality, so boss, chuck this thing out there again.

But yes, I did think removing these leaves trumped this dog's obsessions, so I ignored him, but no good. He found a piece of cordwood, the split kind with sharp corners, and dropped it on my foot. Saying unkind things, I pretended to heave it over toward the west fence line, but didn't let go. I watched him streak off toward the setting sun. While he raced that way I heaved it eastward into the brambles. He searched the west end for a few minutes, then moved south, then east, and finally discovered the log and wrestled it out of the brambles. That gained me ten peaceful minutes.

I couldn't tell whether it disturbed his sense of logic that a west-heaved log ended up in the eastern brambles. At least it bought me a little work time. He was ready to go again, though, and I tried the same ploy. It didn't work the second time. He learned something and waited to see the log actually leave my hand. Fortunately he didn't retain the learning overnight, however, for the next day the first false throw sent him merrily westward.

Raking gives me time to think, so I think about what it's like being Jocko, willing to devote so much time and energy to searching for what's important—but searching everywhere except where it is.

In searching for meaning in a given passage in the Bible, I have discovered that I can find some of its meaning in the passage itself, but I can't get its whole meaning until I have considered how it comports with (1) the meaning of the Bible as a whole (God creates, humankind alienates; nonetheless, God invites us back) and (2) the one fitting response to this extraordinary gift of agape (love God…love self…love neighbor).

Now I invite you to consider what that might mean to you in your own life. You may find it rewarding to do this now, and then again after pondering the concept of God offered in the next chapter. And yet again after you've finished the chapter on living a retrieval spirituality.

Chapter Seventeen

A Concept of the Biblical God

In the first chapters, we found the deity of nature and causation as a concept, a logical construct, a reality derived through reasoning, a transcendent creator God.

From the biblical plot, by contrast, we have seen God interacting with the people, immanent, exhibiting personal character traits. And we have seen that God's character has one predominant trait—a willingness to exercise nonetheless agape—love that has no bounds and no conditions.

But that's not all. Moving now beyond the biblical plot, we can look through the Bible and find other interesting attributes of God.

Other Attributes of God

Various places in the Old Testament show us (1) Yahweh, the creator of all; (2) a force called in Hebrew *ruach* and translated wind, breath of God, life-giving spirit; and (3) a force called in Hebrew *hokmah*, which provides the order and good sense in the universe, translated into English and personified as Wisdom.

Various places in the New Testament show us (1) a transcendent Father; (2) Jesus, the man from Nazareth; (3) Jesus the risen Christ; (4) an attribute of God called the *logos*, which creates the order in the universe; (5) a force which is in Greek *sophia*, translated as "wisdom" and more or less corresponding to the Old Testament's *hokmah*, "wisdom";

and (6) a vital spirit called *pneuma*, used with a meaning similar to *ruach*.

Yahweh/Father

The characteristics of Yahweh from the Old Testament and Father from the New Testament share enough features that we can describe them as a single concept.

We see Yahweh/Father as the creator, the deity who calls people from insignificance, like Abraham and Moses, and puts them to work. This powerful figure vanquishes Pharaoh and his legions, extracting an entire ethnic group from extermination labor, speaks Law and makes it stick, drags his people through forty years of purgation, and finally gives them milk, honey, and dominion over a fertile land.

This Yahweh of the patriarchs, kings, and prophets has a voice to shatter rock and dissension. This muscular deity with irresistible will and boundless means continues into the New Testament as a Father yearning deeply for reunion with the wayward children—even becoming incarnate to live among them to show them firsthand how to love beyond measure and without condition, commissioning ordinary people like Joseph of Nazareth, Peter the fisherman, and Paul the rabbi to go forth to do mighty jobs. This tender Father, as we have seen, welcomes even the most prodigal home.

Wisdom/Sophia/Logos

In the so-called "wisdom literature" in the Old Testament, such as Psalms and Proverbs, *hokmah* is credited not only with instilling, at creation, the order and the wisdom of the universe but also providing counsel for how to live a life faithful to Yahweh, as in this vivid picture of Wisdom calling to the townspeople, "Come, eat of my bread and drink of the wine I have mixed. Lay aside immaturity, and live, and walk in the way of insight." (Prov. 9:5–6, NRSV)

This tradition continues in the New Testament, but now the term changes to the Greek *sophia* but is still translated "wisdom." Paul, for example, calls "Christ the power of God and the wisdom of God" (1 Cor. 1:24, NRSV), thus linking Christ to *sophia*, also shown as a creating force in the universe. And this linkage reinforces a concept that the evangelist John voices when he opens his Gospel with the Greek concept of the *logos*, which creates and orders the universe.

These ideas of the forces behind creation—*hokmah*, *sophia*, and *logos*—must bring to mind the God of causation working through the big bang.

Personally, I am struck with how that creator deity of the big bang/first cause provides an explanation for creation from the rational, scientific, mathematical direction, and those attributes of God called *hokmah*, *sophia*, and *logos* provide an explanation from the biblical direction.

For me, that narrows the distance between the claims of science and the claims of religion to the vanishing point, to a junction of the two. To me it's like saying, "We saw Jocko," and "We saw the Bryans' yellow Lab." No difference but the terms.

Ruach/Pneuma

We are accumulating a rich composite of ideas about God. We turn now to two more, similar to each other in function. They capture the life-giving, sustaining attribute of God.

Genesis tells us that a wind blew over the first waters of creation. The Hebrew for this "wind" is *ruach*. Also, God breathed life into the first of humankind. The Hebrew for this divine breath is also *ruach*. In the New Testament Greek, the corresponding word is *pneuma*, spirit—but plainly related to breath and air, as in our uses in "pneumonia" and "pneumatic." In John 20, the resurrected Christ breathes upon the gathered disciples, imparting to them the new life of God.

I expressed a notion in an earlier chapter that a certain hominid, once upon a time, had a little moment of evolution that developed the very first concept, the distinctive marker of humankind. Perhaps we could consider that the work of *ruach/pneuma*.

God—Yahweh/Father, *hokmah, sophia, logos, ruach/pneuma*. For me, this resembles the work of the big bang/first cause.

Jesus of Nazareth, Incarnate Logos

Our portrayal of the biblical God gets yet more complex when we take up Jesus.

The data are clear enough—a baby was born, grew up, lived his life, was murdered, was resurrected. Meanings are far from clear. The Bible gives us interwoven dimensions to sort through. We find that Jesus the living human being has two complementary offerings:

First, Jesus enacts the policies of God. In the show-and-tell pattern, that's the "show."

Second, Jesus expresses counsel, in the form of universal wisdom, for how to emulate God's policies. In show-and-tell, that's the "tell."

But Jesus has another stratum. The evangelist John, as I said above, identified Jesus as the incarnation of the *logos*, related to *hokmah* and *sophia*, so we add that to Jesus's resume.

And yet more in this figure. After Jesus dies in crucifixion and then resurrects, we encounter the risen Christ, progenitor of the Body of Christ, a way of understanding the continuation of Jesus's work in the world, commonly referred to as the Church.

Jocko Can Be Had

When I picked up my car keys, Jocko came running to find out whether he would be going too. If I pulled on a suit jacket, that would be bad news. Enormous field Labs don't go where suit jackets go. But if I pulled on my parka, "Woof!" He seemed to know we'd be going to the woods.

When I pulled on the bad-news suit jacket, I would call him into the kitchen to be confined, and he would give me his break-your-heart long face, the mournful eyes, the droopy ears, slathering guilt on me. You're leaving me. I can't stand it. I need to be with you.

That was the way it was until I made a small change in the routine. After that, he would run into the kitchen and take his place on his bed, practically urging me to hurry up and leave. Why? Because I had gotten smart. I would get out half a dog biscuit and put it on his bed and command, "Jocko, sit. Jocko, wait." And Jocko would sit and wait, drooling heavily, gazing at the biscuit. Then as I closed the door, I would say, "All right!" and he would gobble it. After a few of these experiences, he didn't bother to come to the closet door. He got on his bed to wait for the dog biscuit. Jocko deliberately exchanged companionship with his friend for the easy gratification of one-half a dog biscuit. That didn't make a lot of sense.

It wasn't as though he had given up enjoying a walk, or enjoying our companionship. It was just that the instant dog-biscuit gratification had higher priority than the delayed gratification.

I Can Be Had

By the time Judy and I married, I had absorbed the concept of God that prevailed in our culture. It was drawn from Bible stories. It was pretty shallow with a stereotype of a white-haired old Caucasian running things.

It offered easy gratification—no complexities, no mysteries, and no enigmas. No requirement to consider the interrelationships of Yahweh/Father, *hokmah, sophia, logos*, Jesus, or *ruach/pneuma*. No challenge to figure out how nonetheless agape could work in actual practice.

This complex of attributes adds up to a powerful concept of God. Taking it all in is not easy. I can't look at it and just think, *Oh, of course, I understand that.*

It's enough to make me yearn for that easier dog biscuit of a concept, the one that's right there within reach and makes me sit down and miss the opportunity to walk with the full-fledged, multilevel God of the Bible, enigmatic, paradoxical, elusive, gripping, compelling, and amazing.

Reflection, Discussion, and Further Quandaries

What are the attributes of your concept of God?

Fourth Quandary

RETRIEVAL SPIRITUALITY

What, We May Well Wonder,
Makes Up Any Spirituality?

Chapter Eighteen

What Is Spirituality?

We've seen a good deal of Jocko retrieving. Now it's time to explain the retrieval spirituality that he helped me develop.

Jocko's Spirituality

Jocko had two yearnings: to eat everything edible and to fetch anything thrown. He found ultimate reality in whatever or whoever provided for those yearnings. That reality was Judy and me: Judy fed him, and I threw sticks for him. Over time, as he discovered our steadfast fidelity to him, he elevated us to be his deities. He was committed to us. Whether he saw us as two separate deities or as one deity in two persons, I couldn't say. He deified us. And what did Jocko do about his deities? He lived a life of fidelity to us, fidelity to his genetic calling to retrieve, fidelity to the value of companionship, and fidelity to his food bowl.

Or, stated otherwise—Jocko was committed to something beyond himself (Judy and me) and Jocko did something about his commitment; he lived it. So we could say that Jocko had a personal spirituality—central convictions and chosen practices. I suppose these were "religious" in the sense that anything done faithfully and conscientiously is done "religiously."

Your Spirituality

Anyhow, your spirituality need not be religious as in believing in God or going to church. Your deep convictions, which you "religiously" act upon and make an integral part of your life, make up your spirituality. So, your spirituality will have, first, a set of convictions, commitments, values, and principles that you freely affirm for yourself ("What I believe") and second, a set of practices, habits, regimens, and behaviors that actualize those values ("What I do about it"). Here are two examples:

A young mother may say, "It's vitally important to me to rear an honest child." This is her commitment to a conviction. It's different from thinking that a child will just grow up honest if left alone. She may continue, "So I find ways to show the difference between honest and dishonest." This is what she's doing about it. Taken together, these two statements form part of her spirituality.

A man working in a large corporation may say, "As far as I'm concerned, the corporate world is a jungle in which the fittest survive and the others go under." That's a deep conviction widely shared. He tells what he does about it: "So whenever I get a chance to take out a competitor, I do it to him before he does it to me." That's part of his "spiritual" practice.

But, I hear the objection: these are not "spiritual," they're secular. I reply that I see no difference. Both express their deep convictions—what they believe—and what they do about them. Obviously this can get trivial. If you believe in brushing your teeth with your left hand rather than your right hand, that's not significant enough to be part of your spirituality. But what you do about child rearing or corporate practices certainly is significant. Over time, it influences what sort of person you are and what impact you have on our life together.

So, spirituality: "Here I stand" and "Here I go."

Reflection, Discussion, and Further Quandaries

Trying to decide "where I stand" and "where I'm going" can be a major challenge. Here is a dichotomy that could provide some answers:

I call to the big dog, "C'mon, Jocko, let's go out and play!" He rises up, big paws and powerful legs getting under him, getting traction, hefting his huge body upright, ears at attention, goofy smile, and tail sweeping. Gangway! Beast coming through! He skids to a stop at the door.

Other dogs—son Alex's or daughter Molly's—arrive at the doorway about the same time, so we might have eight or twelve or sixteen paws agitating for me to spring this starting gate, which I do, and they all take off, clattering through shoulder to shoulder, barking, howling, racing down the deck steps neck and neck into the yard, along the fence, side by side, and round and round.

All except Jocko, who also crashes out of the door onto the deck but then stops, wheels around, and eyes me as if to say, "Yes? What next?" He waits for direction. The interesting thing here is the two differing natures of these dogs. Alex and Molly's dogs have hound bloodlines that send them out to the perimeter to check for intruders and for scent trails that need following. They tend outward. Jocko tends inward.

Centrifugal force versus centripetal force. I reflect on centrifugal forces in our spiritual lives, the desires that pull us away from God (our center point), the distractions that spin us out, and the alienation that drives us from the center point outward.

I reflect on the centripetal forces, our yearnings for communion and God's invitation to communion that draw us closer, center our lives, and place us nearer to the warmth and security of love and grace.

I grieve at the centrifugal forces that separate us, the disputes that threaten yet more schisms in the already divided Body of Christ, and the forces that declare monopolies on truth and exclude the unclean.

My reading of the Gospels shows Jesus beckoning, gathering, and welcoming. His life seems to draw in those outside. I see him inviting those whom the Pharisees have declared unclean. In short, his policies seem centripetal. I think God's must be also.

I smack our tetherball and send it into centrifugal orbit around the pole. God's agape, like the line securing the tetherball to the pole, holds us from flying into outer darkness and, with each revolution, draws us in until we snug up close to our center point and rest, still and secure.

What centrifugal forces in your life draw you outward? Where is outward for you? What centripetal forces draw you inward? Where is inward for you? What bearing does God's grace-love-agape have, if any, on the centrifugal and centripetal forces in your life?

Where do you stand? Where are you going, inward toward God, or outward?

Chapter Nineteen

A Concept of God

It's time now to acknowledge that our two concepts of God are one. The transcendent, causative God and the immanent biblical God constitute one living God. Henceforth, therefore, my use of the word God contains all the meanings we've discovered in the causative God and in the biblical God. We move now to explore how these two attributes of the living God work together in unity.

The Ecology of Jocko

On our deck, we keep a large pottery jar with a brim wide enough for Jocko, one afternoon, to get his head inside and a depth deep enough

for Jocko's head to disappear as he tried to retrieve the throwing stick he had smelled in the bottom. He presented a comic vision so vivid that, after we stopped laughing, I reflected on what I had seen—jarhead Jocko, headless Jocko, and Jocko-body alone.

From his neck down, I saw that Jocko's body consists of a skeletal structure, containing his digestive tract and anchoring his leg bones together with their associated ligaments and muscles. It's all encased in lean meat, mostly musculature, and covered with a skin and fur combo that stops brambles, insulates against icy cold, and has no evident pain receptors. The combined dynamic unit does two things: it digests nourishment to power the whole system, and it propels the entire dog at breakneck velocities out to where he can retrieve. Jocko's body reveals a fine system, each part working in accord with the others, an ecology of dog body.

Jocko Is to His Body as God Is to Transcendence

I could see an analogy between Jocko's body (separate from his head) and God's causation. Just as Jocko's body works efficiently, so God's causation works efficiently, like clockwork, balancing all the forces of nature in an ecology of causes and effects. And just as Jocko's body enables him to fulfill his potential as retriever, so does God, through potentials, fulfill all that ever becomes real. In Jocko's body, as in God's system, we witness marvelous power.

It's the power of interdependence, the multiplier that produces more effect from symbiotic relationships than the sum of their parts. It's the power in a gestalt.

Jocko, Are You Still There?

Eventually Jocko gave up trying to withdraw his head while gripping the stick. In this physics-bound world, the stick-and-head dimensions were larger by far than the head-alone dimensions. I suppose he was running out of oxygen in that enclosed space and knew enough to give up retrieving for a while to emerge and breathe.

Jocko Is to His Head as God Is to Immanence

While Jocko staggered about taking on fresh air, I reflected on this head of his. It, too, had a skeletal structure, a skull to house brain, nose, eyes, and ears and to anchor his jaws with their fine teeth, droopy jowls, and slobbery tongue. The combined dynamic unit inspired me, but I wondered about its interior, namely, Jocko's brain. From that brain sprang all that connected Jocko to us—his wants, needs, personality, character, and responses. To the extent Jocko had any policies, his came

from the consciousness in his brain. His program—smile, wag, beg, greet, eat, sleep, and fetch—all got their signals from his brain.

Just so does the composite Godhead stay connected to us, interacting, present in spirit.

A Coalescence of Jocko

I considered the entire Jocko, his size twenty-two neck fastening his head to his body. The head gets to command the body, "Go that way, now, faster!" The body gets to provide locomotion, acceleration, turning, and braking. The head gets to say, "Start your skid now, you fool, or we'll all die." The body gets to make that happen. These two attributes of Jocko collaborate.

The Living God

I considered two interactive attributes of God: one, like Jocko's body, the universal driving force, the causative attribute; and two, like Jocko's head, the personal, relational attribute. As we imagine God coordinating these two attributes, we admire causation laying down things as they are, systematic, scientific, predictable, reliable, and functioning on schedule.

And we admire what we can imagine God saying through the plot of the Bible: I created you, dear ones, and I wept when you fell into alienation. I called you home, over and over, but you persisted, poor prodigals, in squandering my love. Nonetheless, I did not condemn you or abandon you (read the story), I kept calling and I will keep calling, even after your mortal death, to invite you into communion. I hope you'll accept.

And we glimpse the justice of God emerging from these two attributes—one reckoning, the other beckoning. Both have the absolute power of God driving them, the irresistible force of love against the immovable logic of causation. Living in this paradox, we cannot possibly understand how it works. We can only say, yes.

Hardwired for Love

One crisp fall morning, I decided to walk up a nearby suburban hill and to let Jocko carry a tennis ball. It would, I reasoned, focus him, give him a purpose, and reduce his yearning to retrieve every stick in the gutter and every fluttering leaf. Then I figured that if one tennis ball would focus him a little, two would focus him a lot.

We approached the busy road. I pulled on my heavy gloves, cinched up his leash to its shortest length, and got a two-handed grip on the handle. Battle stations. We got to the intersection. I commanded, "Sit, sir. Down, you big lump." He looked at me with a goofy smile, comical with the tennis balls bulging and tail wagging. Commuter traffic streamed by. I pushed his rump down to sitting and kept the leash taut. Jocko gazed longingly at the other side. At a break in the traffic, we moved out smartly. We got halfway across and were doing fine; the tennis balls kept him focused.

Then Jocko saw a cat sitting on the far curb. His retrieval genes kicked in. He dropped his tennis balls and lunged toward the cat. Then he remembered the tennis balls, but they were rolling into the traffic. We had a conflict of urges: retrieve the tennis balls, the cat, or both?

Cars were bearing down on us. Jocko got to choose because Jocko had 5,000 dog power, four-wheel drive, and high-traction treads. I didn't. He went for the tennis balls first. I went along, willy-nilly. I heard horn blasts from some cars, tires braking from others.

After a while it all got sorted out. The cat had his amusement and walked off. We continued our walk to the hill, and I reflected on "what it all means."

It means that we came close to sudden death. It also means that Jocko hasn't the good common sense to put survival ahead of retrieval, or that he is so hardwired for retrieval that retrieval simply overrides survival, or that he will sacrifice himself if that's what it takes to retrieve the lost balls and the cat.

That's a way of understanding Jesus—so hardwired for love that if he's got to sacrifice everything to invite us back, so be it. When you start to understand Jesus, you start to understand God; it turns out that God is so hardwired for love that no cost is too dear. We will get back these tennis-ball people rolling into the death-dealing traffic even at the risk of personal life, Jesus's life, the life that incarnates God.

Jocko Retrieves Things as God Retrieves People

The analogy gives us a starting place. God retrieves with the same steadfast determination as Jocko retrieves. Things about Jocko's retrieval policy that parallel God's retrieval policy include: searching patiently; enduring any environment where the balls might be found (ice floes in the frozen river, sun-baked suburban asphalt, sharp gravel, or brambles); not giving up during the search on account of cut paws or crucified Son; handling the balls, when found, gently in a gentle mouth; and willing to go back over and over.

Things about Jocko's retrieval policy that I think do not parallel God's retrieval policy include: willing to go back over and over, yes, but (unlike God) at some point running out of energy and becoming a mere collapsed, panting beast; dropping the retrieved balls unceremoniously on the ground then prancing around, tossing them into the air until I give in and chuck them back out; leaving a disgusting slobber all over the balls.

Jocko retrieves something so that he can retrieve it again. God intends the retrieval to be permanent.

The Most Important Difference

Here is the most important difference between Jocko's retrieval policy and God's retrieval policy: Jocko gives the thing to be retrieved no choice in the matter. If he can heft it in those jaws, it will be coming back. If it's stuck in the muck, it will be dragged loose and hauled in.

I think God's retrieval policy is entirely different: God seeks us out, makes contact, and invites us to return to communion, welcoming us when we do. That's different from finding us out there out of communion and coercing or bribing or scaring us till we come in. No, I think we get the invitation and we accept or decline. This policy leaves the responsibility where it belongs, with the individual whose free will God respects and protects. We have liberty to make any choice we wish. When it comes to returning to communion, God neither places barriers in the way nor applies coercion or blandishment.

So our choice, together with the personal responsibility for the consequences of our choice, remains ours and ours alone. Choose.

I Invite Jocko to Come In

Jocko always enjoyed riding in our flat-bottom boat, his front feet up on the sides, ears flapping in the wind, checking out the ducks and geese.

That wasn't half the fun, however, of actually going in the water. On a certain dawn, Jocko and I walked the woods trail along the Potomac, watching the sun come up over Maryland. A freezing northeaster had been blowing these last few January days, kicking up waves that had broken the ice into small, jagged floes. They lapped over one another like miniature tectonic plates jumbled along the beach.

Jocko wasn't at all interested in this scientific simile or the wildness of the river and its arctic wind. Jocko was interested in retrieving the piece of driftwood I had picked up if only I would throw it out where he could fulfill his nature.

I, however, had been reading about training Labradors. A well-trained Lab will sit on command and wait, no matter what, until commanded to fetch. A well-trained Lab will also take guidance in searching, like, "Go right!" or "Back this way!" or "C'mon in."

I commanded, "Jocko, sit." Jocko sat. He knew this hastened the throwing. "Wait." He thought this command was pointless. I lofted the stick far out over the waves, over the floes, and well out into the river. "Wait," I repeated, but Jocko had, of course, already charged after it.

His mighty leap carried him over a floe, almost. He crashed onto it, skidding down into the waves. Surging, he forced apart the next two floes in his way. He paddled with strong rhythm, his great head swinging back and forth searching out the errant wood.

Jocko's eagerness presented him with a problem. Since he hadn't waited to see where the stick went, he had the entire river to search. Another problem was that I had carelessly pitched a waterlogged stick, and it had dropped straight to the bottom.

I grew much disquieted. I imagined that Jocko would, indeed, search the entire Potomac River until his heart and sinews collapsed, sending his corpse to the bottom. I could only wait, hoping that he would fetch just anything and come in. He continued doing his duty to find that doggone stick.

He looked tired. I issued a command, in a strong, calm voice designed to assure him that it was all right to come home empty-jawed. "C'mon in, Jocko," I called. I knew he heard me because his ears did that little jig. He didn't come, though. He just kept searching, swimming in grand circles. I put stronger emphasis on the next command, louder and more strident.

With no physical control over the situation—not that I had much to begin with—all I could do was invite this beloved animal to come in from that lethal environment. "Jocko, you're out there in the floes," I said to myself, "your natural habitat by breeding. You have liberty to do whatever you want. Take it not as license to overfill your destiny, dear dog. Dear dog, turn back. C'mon in."

I considered going after him but then I considered hypothermia and life expectancy, and I did nothing except reflect on how Jocko's free will gave him complete latitude to stay put or come here. And that image called to mind God's predicament: a planet full of people, beloved children, who are busy exercising their God-given liberty, their free will, paddling around in the ice floes of an indifferent natural environment, heedless of invitations to return. What, I wondered, would it be like to be inviting them in—some not hearing, some hearing but otherwise occupied, some trying but unable to get through the floes, and some too confused to know which way to swim?

God Invites Us to Come In

Since the living God of retrieval does not constrain our freedom of will, we can respond to any situation any way we wish. Such freedom of choice plainly lays a heavy burden of responsibility on us, but that is both the beauty and the pain of living under the God-ship of our retrieval God. We get to choose. The constant in the equation is God's persistent, gentle invitation and open welcome.

Fortunately, Jocko did get tired of his obsession. He found a piece of floating driftwood about the size of a toothbrush and came stroking to shore, shoving aside large floes. At one point he decided that a treasure rested on the bottom, and he made a futile dive for it, coming up with the substitute stick only. Majestically he strode ashore, giving a massive shake that sprayed me with muddy Potomac River water, dropping the stick, and looking expectantly for…another throw. He was back in communion with me.

Retrieval to Communion with God

The word communion is usually associated with the liturgical communion service in worship, but I'm using it here for a spiritual condition associated not with liturgy but with being in the spiritual presence of God.

It seems to me indisputable that we all suffer a measure of alienation from God and from one another; alienation seems to be the unavoidable consequence of living. The biblical plot shows that God grieves our loss of communion; but it also shows that God nonetheless invites us to return to communion.

It appears to be an open-door policy. God evidently extends the invitation to communion unconditionally, leaving the decision up to us, individually. We choose to accept or decline. God does not decide for us. You and I stand before the open door, deciding whether to accept or decline the invitation. You choose what you choose, I choose what I choose.

Then we die. The invitation remains open. The invitation remains open as much after we die as it does before we die.

Accepting or Declining the Invitation after Death

What am I talking about, that a person dead could hear and respond to this invitation? I don't know, of course, but I can do the same sort of conceptualizing as I did to get to the idea of God in the first place. Something like this:

Each person has a certain reality, consisting of personhood—a distinctive identity—and a body to carry it in. God maintains a relationship with every personhood from the first human being onward. In this relationship, God invites communion. Some people hear and accept. Some hear and don't. Some never hear at all. God's invitation continues; it's a constant.

At death, the molecular body reverts to individual molecules, disconnected but not lost (the conservation of matter). The personhood continues existence, intact. Where? In nowhere, infinity. When? At no time, eternity. It's the big bang's environment.

In our post-mortal state, God continues the same loving relationship with us as before, a relationship of constantly yearning for our communion and constantly inviting us to communion. If a certain person's conditions of mortal life had prevented that person from hearing the invitation, post-mortal life removes that barrier so that the personhood "hears" it and can respond—accept or decline. I think the invitation is so strong that few decline.

This supposition about post-mortal continuation toward communion with God coordinates well with words in the Episcopal Book of Common Prayer, which ask that the person who has died may "go from strength to strength" and have "continual growth in God's love and service."[20]

This concept has two features: it affirms that God continues to invite us onward, and it places the responsibility for accepting or declining the invitation directly upon each person competent to make a decision.

Regarding those not competent to decide—the children, those mentally or physically ill-equipped to handle the concepts, those who have never heard of any of this at all, including those who lived before any of this ever came up for discussion—I am confident that the living God will have a loving policy, a nonetheless policy.

Moreover, Jesus's parable tells us that the prodigal son, thoroughly alienated from his father, heard, in some interior way, an invitation to return. He had liberty to choose to accept or to decline. He chose to accept and take responsibility for whatever consequences flowed from that choice. His father held out an unconditional welcome home.

Jesus told this story to let us know how we are with God. It tells me that God, despite any level of our alienation, retrieves by an invitation always extended, which we can voluntarily accept or decline.

This idea of retrieval springs partly from the meaning of the Bible when it is read as a whole plot: creator God creates us in communion, shalom; we alienate from God and one another. Nonetheless, God in agape invites us to return to communion, shalom.

It springs partly from Jesus's encounter with death that led to resurrection, for the resurrection itself serves as retrieval. That is, death alienated the mortal Jesus from his people, his work, and his program; nonetheless, God created a new reality in which those separated from Jesus were invited to return to his work and his program, to become the Body of Christ making God's program of retrieval real in their world.

Anyhow, I like the idea of God's policy of retrieval. How it actually works I will discover as I leave this mortal condition. Until then, it seems right.[21]

Shalom

I have used the term communion to designate a condition close to God and congruent with God's policies. Here I take that to the next stage.

In the chapters regarding causation, the big bang, and transcendence, I said that the initial conditions of the big bang were in perfect equilibrium, which corresponded to the ancient Hebrew concept of shalom. If shalom names a universal precondition, if it permeates the nature of nature and all that has been and is being created, I am willing to say that it also characterizes the end-state, the end-times, the last day, and the end of time. If God created our universe and us in shalom, perhaps shalom would also be the ultimate condition of fulfillment, of communion. In John's Gospel, Jesus's last word was *tetelesthai*—it is finished, completed, fulfilled, accomplished. Shalom.

God's Retrieval Policy during Mortal Life

That all applied to retrieval after death. I think it works just as much during our lifetimes in experiences that closely resemble actual crucifixion and resurrection.

Again, the prodigal son provides the template. We can interpret the death of the prodigal's home life and his relationship with his father as an event so calamitous as to resemble a crucifixion. And we can interpret his return to a new and different condition as a resurrectional event, for new life has emerged from the deathliness of the old life.

I am not talking about "things came out all right after all—it rained on our picnic, but we saw a great movie instead." I am talking about substantial rearrangements in the spiritual condition.

For example, imagine what's going on in these statements: "After they failed me and I became disillusioned about their project, I made some serious changes and found a new serenity and approach to life." Or, "the couple became alienated, but after careful efforts they found reconciliation and a new way to relate to each other." Those are modest everyday examples of the resurrectional proceeding from experience resembling crucifixion.

I think God has built this dynamic into the universe, a potential originally loaded into the big bang to become a functioning reality.

To Summarize

What convictions emerge from all this? Personally, I keep trying to get a grip on God our creator, whose nonetheless retrieval policy invites me to communion, shalom. The concept, spanning the vastness of big-bang origins and infinite potential, the tender love displayed in the biblical narrative, the optimism of the New Creation, and the attraction of final shalom—well, it's overwhelming. Finding a worthy response looms as the next step in our retrieval spirituality.

Reflection, Discussion, and Further Quandaries

As you prepare to bridge from this long-winded analysis of how things are between God and us, please consider a dream I had.

In my dream, Jocko was sleeping soundly on the kitchen floor just in front of the fridge when an object landed smack on his head. It was a loaf of bread that one of us had carelessly pitched up there for temporary storage. Maybe vibration from the motor of the fridge had gradually slipped it closer to the edge until it dropped off. Anyhow, it did, right onto Jocko's head.

Jocko opened his eyes to see a midnight snack. "Manna from heaven!" said he. And then he stood up, straightened himself into a moral stance, and declared in perfect Lab-speak, "No, I shall not avail myself of this unearned opportunity to gorge. This bread does not belong to me but to the household gods, sound asleep and depending upon me to guard their assets. I shall return to my snooze, on alert." He nosed the loaf to a safe spot and lay back down.

When I woke up and recollected this fantasy, I had a hearty laugh, imagining our opportunistic dog exercising any restraint whatsoever when it came to eating anything that came along, whether given, stolen, or dropped from the heavenly fridge.

Just so do I cast a skeptical eye on the likelihood that the world will adopt my idea of living a life of nonetheless responses and nonetheless agape. Such a life calls for restraint on self-interest, dedication of self to the greater good, and centering one's life on serving God.

Some people do actually live this way, do live lives of genuine, heart-felt service. (Let me stipulate here that I am talking not about marquee lives like Mother Teresa's and Mahatma Gandhi's, but the ordinary lives of ordinary folks, everyday lives of honesty, decency, service, and caring.) But others spend their lives making the bad news on the front page of the newspaper—venality, cruelty, selfishness, power-grabbing, maliciousness, exploitation; it's all there—monumental alienation.

Nonetheless, I say again, opportunities to emulate the policies of God as enacted by Jesus are right in front of us, ready to translate into practice. I struggle with this.

I think one habit of mind gets in my way, my habit of thinking about my choices in terms of what I can get away with, my childish way of looking over my shoulder to see whether anyone is watching before going for the cookie jar. It's my habit of governing my life by law instead of grace. Of course I won't try it if someone is watching, and of course I can contrive some clever way of getting away with it. Those aren't the issues. The issues are whether or not reaching into the cookie jar emulates the policies of God enacted by Jesus. That sounds pretty high-minded, but it also sounds adult.

The bar is set high. But it's a bar of grace, not law.

So, reflecting on all this and preparing to see what comes next in our retrieval spirituality, what do you think?

Perhaps you are reacting against my notion of nonetheless agape since it seems so contrary to nature and habit, such an invitation to exploitation. Yes? No? The next chapter deals with these concerns.

Chapter Twenty

Life in Retrieval Spirituality

One day I was trying to decide between a hard commitment and an easy dodge. It got me to wondering how Jocko would handle this dilemma in his own fields of interest—food and retrieving. So, out on the deck I picked up a handful of Kibbles and a tennis ball. Jocko watched with keen eyes, drooling mouth, and quivering nose. I held both hands high, out of reach but not sight. He acted frantic, leaping and woofing.

Then I did a cruel thing. I pitched the ball out into the yard. As he started to lunge for the steps, he spied me putting the Kibbles onto the deck. He saw the ball rolling into the honeysuckle. He saw the Kibbles at my feet. He froze. This poor dog suffered a paralytic dilemma—fetch or eat?

He had free will. He could do either, but not both at once. Finally the Kibbles, closer, easier, and swifter to gratify, won out. He inhaled them and headed for the tennis ball. It was the end of my experiment, but not the end of teasing out the meaning in it.

Jocko did not need the nourishment of those Kibbles. He was not starving. He wanted them because they gratified his perpetual appetite. Gratification lay within lunge-distance with no strain, no cost, no investment, and no commitment. On the other hand, retrieving the tennis ball would require effort, a mad dash down the steps and into the brambles, and snuffling about. Work.

Cheap Grace, Costly Grace

I have to choose, regularly, between the easy dodge and the hard commitment. In the easy dodge, I think to myself, Jonathan, you don't need to go to all that trouble. Remember our retrieval spirituality, the welcome news that our living God has infinite patience with you, that regardless of how irresponsible you are, God's nonetheless policy will always forgive and God will be waiting there for you to celebrate your return. Take it easy; you deserve a break today.

Familiar words, always mouthed with deep sincerity and full-strength rationale. I'm tired, I did some good stuff just last week; it's only this once, and so forth. What's grace good for if you can't enjoy it? Does the living God really express agape or is that just an advertising slogan?

In answer, I turn to the example of Dietrich Bonhoeffer, a German Lutheran pastor who began denouncing Hitler's Nazism from the beginning of its climb to dominance in the early 1930s. He became an influential voice for those who opposed the Nazi policies leading to the Holocaust. Able to speak more freely from London, he spent two years there, 1933–1935, but then made a fateful decision by returning to Nazi Germany to continue to strive against the evil.[22]

If he had not made that decision, the Nazis could not have imprisoned him in 1943, nor could they in 1945 have hanged him by the neck until he was dead. But he did make that decision, and they did hang him. His decision enacted what he had been writing, teaching, and preaching about all those years, what he called costly grace.

The living God, wrote Pastor Bonhoeffer, freely offers boundless grace and infinite love. That's wonderful, but it also tempts us to exploit the gift and to do any little thing our hearts desire, knowing that the nonetheless policies of God will let us off the hook. He called this cheap grace.[23]

When I think that God's grace will relieve me of responsibility and I deliberately do or say something unworthy, I exploit grace, I grasp cheap grace. When I know that what I am about to do will sadden my friend, but I do it anyhow because I also know that my friend forgives readily, I am exploiting grace, grasping cheap grace. How easy life can be if not lived under threat of penalty or consequential accountability. Why bother to comply with the law if the police have been laid off and court is never in session?

Pastor Bonhoeffer urged costly grace—responding to the gift of gracious love with gracious love, not taking advantage of it but emulating it. And he went to certain death as an act of costly grace.[24]

The Harder, Not Easier, Response

I recognize that this walk through the quandaries has brought us to a concept of the living God that seems to invite us to exploit gracious love, agape, and nonetheless policies. It invites notions that the living God is a sort of push-over, an indulgent figure with loose standards.

It may appear to be a gospel of affirmation, not transformation, presenting a "benign divine," everyone's pal. Some will complain that it is long on tolerance and short on accountability, or long on forgiveness and short on sin. Some will note that it mentions salvation not at all, nor morality, and that it favors the grace of God and God's love, ignoring the God of justice and God's wrath.

One could indeed decide that the object of life is to get away with as much as possible. For this purpose, our retrieval spirituality could appear to be the perfect dodge.

But one could also choose to live a harder way, a more demanding way, and decide that the object of life is to emulate God's policies as closely as possible. I find it much harder to do what's right when no one is looking. I might think I'm getting away with a lot, but there may be a better way, something like costly grace and the tough commitment to responding to nonetheless agape not with exploitation of grace but with further nonetheless agape.

Revisiting the Central Meaning of the Bible

In the chapter on finding the central meaning of the Bible, I concluded with this:

"Yes, God created all in equilibrium and yes, humankind alienated themselves from God and one another, and yes, God nonetheless invited humankind to return to communion; therefore yes, I can think of but one fitting response to this extraordinary gift of agape: love God…love self…love neighbor. There it is. The gold standard. A biblical conclusion that can give direction to life. I could adopt it as my own spiritual constitution."

But I get exasperated with unassailable generalities like that, especially pieties that look great but have no evident application. Let's revisit this one to see whether it offers anything actually useful.

Living a God-Centered Life

How exactly will I love God…love self…love neighbor? An answer emerges from a paraphrase of President Kennedy's inaugural line, "Ask not what God can do for you, but what you can do for God."

One cultural spirituality treats God like a utilitarian godlet, a step-n-fetch-it gofer, the equivalent of those little Baals that so tempted the Israelites in Canaan. This concept of God comes down to a series of prayers like, "God, get me happiness, get me relief from this pest, get me smarts, get me power, get me this, and get me that."

The alternative that attracts me asks not what I can get out of my relationship with God, but what I can give to and do for God's people. This manner of life would use this simple directive: love God, love self, love neighbor.

It would dedicate to God my every thought, every judgment, every act, every decision, and every choice. It would send each one through this filter: does what I am about to think, say, or do express love for God, love for self, and love for neighbor? If yes, think it, say it, and do it. If no, work on it until it does.

I state this not because it's my personal practice but because it is a conceptual standard, a "God-centered life," that I can aspire to. There's not a chance in this world that I could ever meet it. But it's a standard to work with.

Responding to Grace with Grace

Just a note to emphasize what I said about Pastor Bonhoeffer—that he urged us to respond to grace with grace, not exploitation. That makes sense to me. If only I could do it.

It would mean setting up some benchmarks for a nonetheless policy, such as finding means of reconciliation when none seems apparent; adopting grace, not legalisms; promoting unity, not division; finding hope to replace desperation; managing relationships, so far as possible, by covenants (reserving contracts for business); seeking win-win solutions; expanding the circle of people included; trusting in God's economy of abundance; and practicing compassion.

All of which adds up to emulating the God of perpetual creation and nonetheless hospitality. For me, it's a whole lot harder than earning points by staying within clear-cut rules. It requires me to take personal responsibility for living with rigorous spiritual integrity. Good luck.

Farewell to Old Jocko

The morning of Monday, December 16, 2002, started with a grand sunrise shining through the trees in our backyard, Jocko's playground, where he had retrieved maybe seven million tennis balls, several cords of wood, and his old smashed basketball.

Over the weekend, he had stopped eating and was drinking only ice water laced with a bit of chicken broth. The cancer bloated his midriff. He could stand up and stagger outside to void but only with great difficulty. Dr. Farrell, his wonderful veterinarian, had assured us over the past weeks that we would know the right moment and that he would gladly drive to our house to save Jocko the discomfort of coming to his office. Jocko's grave was ready in the woods behind our house.

So all was fulfilled. His life was complete, and he lay on his beloved bed, Judy and I huddled beside him. He still showed no signs of pain, just decline, weakening, and indifference. The big tail did still whack the floor whenever we spoke, but that was about it. We put in the call to Dr. Farrell. Jocko made one last walk to a sunny spot on the floor. Dr. Farrell came. The kind needle sent the great dog off. We carried his body to his grave and completed his presence among us.

Only a dog, but a presence of four-legged love, a constant of joy, of fidelity, of worship, and of friendship…a walking, woofing metaphor for all that's decent about living and loving.

I guess it's the fulfillment that speaks to me about December 16, 2002, and all of that day's images embedded in my memory. Jocko started life in the basement just below where he died, a life already imprinted with potential for loyalty, retrieval, adoration, joie de  vivre, appetite, and communication. He fulfilled these potentials in his years with us. They grew into major assets in our household life. Because he enacted them daily, he encouraged them in us, and his life enhanced our lives, thus fulfilling his life-giving potential.

Warps and Woofs

Just doing what came naturally, Jocko made a big difference to me. On our walks in the woods, I moved along my well-worn trail, throwing sticks for him, sending him crashing through the thickest brambles, fording the iciest streams, galumphing in the muckiest mud holes (he liked to lie down in these), and clawing up the steepest inclines. I walked the trail; Jocko crisscrossed the trail.

Our walking pattern resembled yarns on a loom: some yarns stretch top to bottom (the warp), while the shuttle carries other yarns (the woof) back and forth, over and under the warp. Yes, that's it, I had the well-worn path of conventional thoughts, the warp. Jocko retrieved my stick-quandaries from the rough terrain of unconventional thought, the woof. Thus did Jocko's woof-yarn weave over and under my warp-yarn, his unconventional woof challenging my conventional warp until we wove this new thought-fabric called retrieval spirituality.

I like having a new thought woven out of old thoughts, transforming but not replacing the old. Such is the beauty when old and new coalesce, neither being lost, both being improved.

Coalescence from Warp and Woof

I wish those who promote new approaches to church and political matters would coalesce their ideas with those who cleave to old approaches to church and political matters—and vice versa. As it is, they try to settle the resulting disputes on the model of a football game, the two sides butting heads and making end runs in desperate efforts to reach a goal. When one side reaches the goal, the other side loses. I thought we were all in this predicament of life together.

Why not behave that way, and try the model of the biceps and triceps. These are decidedly opposing muscles, arranged to work against each other so that one can pull the arm up and the other can pull the arm down. Without both, my arms would be in a sorry state. We'd all be in a sorry state if one of these disputing sides should win and the other lose. We need both to discover any useful solutions. The concept of coalescence—two opposing  ideas merging the best of each to yield a new, improved idea: that's what Jocko taught me—warp needs woof.

God Invites Us to Communion

I am moving toward my mortal end. So are you. In this life, we can't possibly fulfill our potential to become fully human. Failure to reach this fulfillment would seem a frightful waste, quite contrary to God's economy of abundance and fulfillment elsewhere in creation.

Here is a way to think about that idea. First, we have noted that God evidently worked through the big bang/first cause to install the potential for humankind to exist and for individual humans to be born and to live and to die. That has happened and is happening.

Second, I think that the trajectory of the Bible's plot demonstrates God's intent to retrieve us (invite us) to final communion, regardless of how we live our lives. God's persistent, steadfast grace repeated over and over in the Bible's plot demonstrates this, no matter how simultaneously comforting and troubling the thought may be when contrasted with conventional truisms.

So it doesn't seem to me that my death, the end of my mortality, will be the end of my process of fulfillment. I don't think the game is over when my heart and breathing stop.

For Jocko, yes. That was it for our old friend. He was just a beast, a terrific beast, but just a beast. My memories of him continue to inspire me. In that sense, he continues to fulfill his potential. But that's it. When I and others who remember him are gone, Jocko will be gone.

Not so for you and me. We will continue, as God's beloved children, creations with potential to be fully human, to be fulfilled. God's invitation to communion—the great retrieval—will remain open.

For like tennis balls in the brambles or rotten sticks vanished under the Potomac, we continue evermore to be the beloved children of the living God who continues evermore to seek us, to retrieve us—if we will.

God Seeks to Retrieve Us If We Will?

That last thought sits there like any number of annoying religious assertions, undocumented and speculative. So I depend upon a certain story that has helped me not only derive the thought itself but also its documentation and rational substance.

It's a story that will sound like a literal account of what actually happened, but I hear it emerging from my cloud of unknowing, from that land where the true supersedes the actual. That's the teacher in me speaking, the student of literary expression.

And the preacher in me declares that this story is true in a transcendent way, that it is a true account in mythic terms of what its underlying historical events signify.

From Death to New Life, New Creation

Anyhow, here it is. At first it won't seem relevant to my idea that God seeks to retrieve us if we will. But eventually it will get there. The story:

As the sun went down on a certain springtime Friday during the Roman occupation of Jerusalem, outside the city walls on a rocky promontory called Golgotha, the Place of the Skull, a bloody cross stood, empty. Nearby lay the corpse of the man who had died nailed to that cross, Jesus of Nazareth.

When Jesus died, he died absolutely. His mortal body ceased living. His brain was dead; his organs were dead. His flesh began to decompose, just as ours will. His death was no different from our death, for he was fully human as well as fully divine. Women had wrapped the corpse with a shroud like swaddling cloths. They had laid it in a cavity hewn from limestone rock resembling the manger of his birth. We see here signs that we are witnessing a new birth emerging from mortal death.

Friday

As to Friday. God, according to the myth, completed genesis (the beginnings) on the sixth and last day, Friday. Some billions of years later, the creation was fulfilled. Remember Jesus's word from the cross: *tetelesthai*, "It is fulfilled." Death on Friday, therefore, signifies the end of the original creation. Why? Because he, Jesus of Nazareth, had been born as the incarnate Word of God, the Logos of God, which John's Gospel said had imparted order and natural law into the universe at creation, just as *hokmah* had done. We see here the God of causation, the God who loaded all causation and all potential into the big bang and let 'er rip. Same God, different accounts.

So when his mortal life ended, the universe, which he had "birthed" at creation, died also. When the sun set on this terminal Friday, both the sixth day and the old creation ended. (That's a statement of mythic, not literal seven-day truth.)

To put this another way, on that Friday, the original creation that had come from nothing, no-thing, a void, returned to nothing, no-thing, a void. When the incarnation of the Logos went down, all went down.

Saturday

Saturday began, the seventh day of creation. All rested in sabbath-time. Saturday ended.

Sunday

On Sunday, the first day of the new week, God did a new creation. A what? The book of Genesis says that a wind, *ruach*, blew over the first waters of creation, and that God's breath, also *ruach*, animated the first of humankind. I want to say that the breath of God, on that first Easter dawn, did what the breath of God did originally, that is, create reality out of nothing. The reality, newly created, was unique, never-before experienced life in Jesus resurrected.

We must linger a moment over this word resurrected. It emphatically does not mean "resuscitated," or "revivified," or "restored," which imply a return to a previous state, or even the same thing done over better. Resurrect must have the unique meaning of create (not "make") something all over again, from scratch, ex nihilo, from nothing, in a new and unique form and structure.

Jesus's molecules didn't reconstitute into Mary's human (and divine) child Jesus—they had been irretrievably deconstructed. They became, instead, resurrected. Yes, there is continuity between Jesus and the risen Christ, for it was Jesus who was resurrected. He was first dead then resurrected into a new creation. In God's once and only resurrection, Jesus became a new—brand new, not refurbished—creation. In the absolute void of the nothingness left when Jesus died dead and gone, God created all things new. From the first day, the first Sunday of the old creation, we have gone to the next Sunday, the first day of the new creation.

We have no touchstone to help us understand this process. It is unique to Jesus. It had never happened before. It happened only once and has never happened since.

Dare we stretch the image yet further to say that inside the tomb on that new Sunday occurred an expansion, a big bang? Remember that in that original big bang in no place, at no time, and with nothing (no thing, no entity, no being) God set forth all creation—manifest in physical form (time, space, energy, natural law, etc.) and spiritual form (all concepts, all potentials). In this big bang of resurrection, God set forth a new creation manifest in physical form (the body of the risen Christ) and spiritual form (the breath, the Spirit of God in the risen Christ). The old has gone. Behold, the new, the risen Christ of God!

From the Body of Jesus to the Body of Christ

When the sun brought light in the east, the women went to the tomb to finish preparing the dead body. They didn't find it, of course, because it belonged to the old creation, now gone, kaput. What they did find, although it took long, hard soul-searching to figure this out, was the Body of Christ. It was, for those next few days, his resurrection body, a transitional reality. The risen Christ took several days to instruct his perplexed friends about who they now were in this new creation. Instruction completed, the risen Christ faded from view.

Crucifixion, Resurrection: Hinge of History

It took me a long time to see the full significance of the story of crucifixion and resurrection. I finally realized that it is the hinge of history: that moment to which all had been leading and from which all has been proceeding when nothing was ever again as it was before.

The Body of Christ

This breath of God, this Spirit of God, this *pneuma* continued to enliven them as new creatures of God just as Genesis explained that *ruach*, the original breath of life, had enlivened humankind in the first place.

They eventually caught on that they had become a new creation, had had a resurrectional experience (not a resurrection) and were now the Body of Christ. They were no longer of the old creation but of the new humankind, the spiritual legacy of the Christ of God, and the reality of God resident in the world.

This, in turn, meant that they embodied the policies of God as Jesus had enacted them—steadfast love, faithful relationships, service to others, care for the needy, and healing the broken. In all ways they were to emulate the policies of God that they had seen and heard in Jesus. This meant that to keep this good news of new creation to themselves would be unworthy, so they got talkative and told everybody what they had experienced.

They began to preach a gospel of hope and new life. Many people throughout the Mediterranean basin responded and were baptized into the Body of Christ.

Baptism into the Body of Christ

Baptism has at least two meanings: first, it replicates the Hebrews' exodus from Egyptian bondage through the Red Sea waters and up into the covenant with Yahweh—that is, it signifies death to the old life of alienation from God and birth into new life with God. So a person goes down into the waters of baptism (some traditions do actual immersion, some apply water symbolically) and "drowns, dies," then comes up from the waters into new life. It's like going down into the Red Sea and up into a new covenant with God and God's people. This meaning honors the ancient Hebrew tradition of exodus from bondage to alienation into a new life with God.

Second, baptism replicates Jesus's mortal death and resurrection into new life. In this way, a person being baptized accepts a death to the old way of life outside the Body of Christ and acknowledges a new life—communion—with a new way of life as a committed member of the Body of Christ, commonly called the Church.

The new Christian communities adopted these meanings of baptism to make a coherent rite of initiation for new members of the Body. They also formulated a creedal affirmation—the Apostles' Creed—as a standardized basis for belief. The problem that arises from this practice centers on theologians' tendency to derive intricate doctrines from the simple affirmations. Inevitable disputes over these doctrines then engender divisions and broken unity. Unity was the central value implicit in the idea of the Body of Christ, that all will be one, not disputing factions.

The Great Commission

The risen Christ did two things for his followers: he commissioned them to go forth into the world to continue the work Jesus had begun, and he endowed them with the Spirit of God, namely, unity, love, mutual concern, and compassion, which empowered them to do this work.

The first small communities of new people gathered in the name of Christ—Christians. On Sunday mornings (the day of resurrection) they gathered and ate together, recalling Jesus's last supper with his disciples. These meals became ways to express love for one another, for God, and for all people—the essence of what Jesus had taught them about God's policies.

At first they called their eating together "agape meals." Soon, however, they considered them sacramental events that manifested the Christ present and real among them. When giving thanks for this experience, they began to call it by the Greek word for thanksgiving—*eucharistia*, the Eucharist. It became a way not only to experience the presence of the risen Christ, but also to experience communion—unity with Christ and with one another.

Communion in the Eucharist projected itself into their everyday lives together, giving them a sense of being one in Christ, unified in their work and in their mutual identities. We are, they said, one body, unified in Christ. All in all, it gave them a way to understand themselves as moving toward communion with God after death.

They identified themselves as the hands, voices, feet, and heart of God living on in the world, a community working to continue what Jesus had begun. It made them One Body, indivisible. Naturally, however, being human folk, they soon began to dispute. Paul had to write to the community in Corinth to tell them to stop all this division and factionalism. You are one in Christ. Do not, do not, divide the Body. (1 Cor. 1:10–15)

Being the Body in Shalom

Against the background of the story of crucifixion, resurrection, new creation, and the Body of Christ, we can discern our own way to live, to structure worthy priorities, and to frame our nonetheless policies. For me, it's a matter of emulating these concepts to the extent that I can figure ways to do that.

As our mortal hearts and minds squirm and maneuver, our perplexing problems and quandaries shift and grow. But a constant remains firmly fixed out there—the living God beyond and within, creating anew, always creating. And under it all, under our lives and our yearnings, lies shalom, our origin, our potential, our destiny, the shalom of God.

Walking with Jocko

A few weeks after Jocko died that winter day, I walked our woods on an overcast morning just before dawn. Hard weather had given the woods a beating. Wind and ice had uprooted trees and broken branches. The creeks were flushing eroded topsoil and suburban run-off. I slogged through the muck of mud, dead leaves, and rotten wood. Death, decay, and brokenness surrounded me.

I missed my walking buddy. I could see him in vivid memory, the water dog having a grand time, chasing his sticks through the bogs and puddles, and lying down to wallow and lap icy water. In his great O-be-joyful-Jubilate-Jocko way, he saw not death, decay, and brokenness, but life to live, fulfilling potential fully, doing what he loved doing, being a loyal companion, fretting not one minute in twelve years.

I called out to him, "What's the deal, Jocko? Look at all these fallen and broken trees and all this mud and rotten wood." The Jocko in my memory paused, gave me a long, thoughtful look, which was a little hard to take seriously with four sticks gripped in those amazing jaws.

I thought I could hear this big, gentle Lab say, "Your problem is that you walk with your eyes down. I know you want to see where you're going, but all you ever see down there is the muck of mud and rotten wood and dead leaves. You get dismayed about climbing over these dead trees, and you begin to think that everything in the woods is dead or dying or rotten. Raise your eyes and look for new life. Notice the green willow sprouts and the reddish maple buds."

Then in my imagination, I watched him return to his obsession, trotting up and down in the muddy stream bed, collecting dead sticks.

I trudged on through the muck but now not so fast, so I could notice a few buds starting to swell, feel the first hint of spring air, and see a ray of rising sun peeping under the overcast. Rotten, yes; nonetheless, spring.

A Last Word

A few years ago I wanted to draw together my thoughts into a little hymn for our congregation to sing. So I wrote the following verses that summarize how I feel about my idea that nonetheless, God retrieves us.

Dear gracious God, we lift our hearts
in grateful worship-love
for all the gifts your grace imparts
to lift our souls above.

Creator God, we dedicate
our lives entire to you
to serve, to give, to celebrate
creation now anew.

Incarnate God, we gather here
in bonded covenant,
as Christ's own Body to revere
your presence jubilant.

Show us, we pray, your way of cross,
Your way of loving grace,
Teach us forgiveness and hard loss
To gain shalom's embrace.

Guide us to serve, to love, to give;
guide us to sacrifice;
guide us to die and rise to live
at resurrection's price.

We seek to grow, O yeasty Lord,
through your own Spirit strong,
into our Christ, creator Word,
long past our evensong.

REFERENCES

Anderson, Bernhard W. *Understanding the Old Testament*. Third edition. Englewood Cliffs, New Jersey, 1975.

Armstrong, Karen. *A History of God: The 4000 Year Quest of Judaism, Christianity and Islam*. New York: Ballentine Books, 1993.

Bonhoeffer, Dietrich. *The Cost of Discipleship*. New York: SCM Press, 1959.

Brown, Raymond E. *A Crucified Christ in Holy Week: Essays on the Four Gospel Passion Narratives*. Collegeville, MN: The Liturgical Press, 1992.

Davies, Paul. *The Mind of God: The Scientific Basis for a Rational World*. New York: Simon and Schuster, 1992.

Dictionary of Christian Theology. Edited by Alan Richardson. Philadelphia: The Westminster Press, 1969.

Discovery Institute, "A Scientific Dissent From Darwinism," http://www.discovery.org.

Griffin-Jones, Robin. *The Four Witnesses: The Rebel, the Rabbi, the Chronicler, and the Mystic*. San Francisco: HarperSanFrancisco, 2000.

Hebbelthwaite, Brian. *The Christian Hope*. Grand Rapids: William B. Eerdmans Publishing Company, 1984.

Holman, Hugh. *A Handbook to Literature*. Indianapolis: The Odyssey Press, 1960.

Macquarrie, John. *Principles of Christian Theology*. New York: Charles Scribner's Sons, 1977.

NASA, "Big Bang Cosmology," http://map.gsfc.nasa.gov/m_uni/uni_101bb1.html.

National Center for Science Education, http://www.ncseweb.org.

New International Dictionary of New Testament Theology. Edited by Colin Brown. Grand Rapids: Zondervan Publishing House, 1971.

Oxford Companion to United States History. Edited by Paul S. Boyer. Oxford: Oxford University Press, 2001.

Phillips, J.B. *Your God Is Too Small.* New York: The Macmillan Company, 1957.

Polkinghorne, John. *The God of Hope and the End of the World.* New Haven: Yale Nota Bene, 2002.

von Balthasar, Hans Urs. *Dare We Hope "That All Men Be Saved"?* Translated by Dr. David Kipp and Rev. Lothar Krauth. San Francisco: Ignatius Press, 1988.

Westminster Dictionary of Church History. Edited by Jerald C. Brauer. Philadelphia: The Westminster Press, 1971.

NOTES

[1] John Macquarrie, *Principles of Christian Theology* (New York: Charles Scribner's Sons, 1977), 71–72. A helpful definition and discussion. See also various articles on sin, depravity, grace, and the like in *A Dictionary of Christian Theology*, ed. Alan Richardson (Philadelphia: The Westminster Press, 1969), and thorough word studies of sin and related concepts in *The New International Dictionary of New Testament Theology*, ed. Colin Brown (Grand Rapids: Zondervan Publishing House, 1971).

[2] Ibid.

[3] Paul Davies, *The Mind of God: The Scientific Basis for a Rational World* (New York: Simon and Schuster, 1992), 189–191.

[4] Karen Armstrong, *A History of God: The 4000 Year Quest of Judaism, Christianity and Islam* (New York: Ballentine Books), 1993, 36–39.

[5] Ibid., 204–208.

[6] *The Oxford Companion to United States History*, ed. Paul S. Boyer (Oxford: Oxford University Press, 2001), 177.

[7] Davies, 72-175

[8] NASA, "Big Bang Cosmology," http://map.gsfc.nasa.gov/m_uni/uni_101bb1.html.

[9] Ibid.

[10] Davies, 61–69. In these pages, and also elsewhere in his book, Professor Davies gives an excellent survey of various approaches to the quandaries regarding the big bang and deity. As a professor of mathe-

matical physics at the University of Adelaide in Australia and a person who has thought long and hard about spiritual matters, he offers wonderful analyses combining the two disciplines.

[11] Ibid. 87–92. Davies has an intriguing explanation of initial conditions.

[12] J.B. Phillips, *Your God Is Too Small* (New York: The Macmillan Company, 1957), 9–69.

[13] Discovery Institute, "A Scientific Dissent from Darwinism," http://www.discovery.org.

[14] The National Center for Science Education, at http://www.ncseweb.org. is one of many scientific organizations resisting the ID movement's efforts to include ID in the science curriculum.

[15] Bernhard W. Anderson, *Understanding the Old Testament*, 3rd ed. (Englewood Cliffs, New Jersey, 1975). This entire book gave me a perspective on the Old Testament that led me to realize that the Bible taken as a whole has a coherent plot.

[16] Robin Griffin-Jones, *The Four Witnesses: The Rebel, the Rabbi, the Chronicler, and the Mystic* (San Francisco: HarperSanFrancisco, 2000), 3–20. The rest of the book develops the idea that each of the four Gospels has its own unique origin and purpose.

[17] Ibid. I have added my own ideas to those of Professor Griffin-Jones.

[18] Raymond E. Brown, *A Crucified Christ in Holy Week: Essays on the Four Gospel Passion Narratives* (Collegeville, MN: The Liturgical Press, 1992), has a splendid study of the unique ways each Gospel presents the crucifixion.

[19] Hugh Holman, *A Handbook to Literature* (Indianapolis: The Odyssey Press, 1960), 396-399 ("Plot"), 173-175 ("Dramatic Structure"), and 118-119 ("Conflict").

[20] *The Book of Common Prayer and Administration of the Sacraments and Other Rites and Ceremonies of the Church, According to the Use of the Episcopal Church* (New York: The Church Hymnal Corporation, 1979), 330 and 481.

[21] Hans Urs von Balthasar, *Dare We Hope "That All Men Be Saved"?*, trans. Dr. David Kipp and Rev. Lothar Krauth (San Francisco: Ignatius Press, 1988); Brian Hebbelthwaite, *The Christian Hope* (Grand Rapids: William B. Eerdmans Publishing Company, 1984); and John Polkinghorne, *The God of Hope and the End of the World* (New Haven and London: Yale Nota Bene, 2002) are all helpful in thinking through these hard questions.

[22] G. Leibholz, "Memoir," in Dietrich Bonhoeffer, *The Cost of Discipleship*, trans. R.H. Fuller (New York: Macmillan Publishing Co., Inc. 1963), 11–35.

[23] Dietrich Bonhoeffer, *The Cost of Discipleship*, trans. R.H. Fuller (New York: Macmillan Publishing Co., Inc., 1963), 45–60.

978-0-595-39583-5
0-595-39583-X

Printed in the United States
69570LVS00006B/181-300

9 780595 395835